THE ALLURE OF
CHARLESTON

THE ALLURE OF
CHARLESTON

HOUSES, ROOMS, AND GARDENS

SUSAN SULLY

RIZZOLI
NEW YORK

New York · Paris · London · Milan

CONTENTS

DEFINING CHARLESTON STYLE

The moment you step into the historic district of Charleston, South Carolina, you know you are in a place unlike anywhere else. Something about its streetscape of pediments and porticoes, white porches, sun-aged plaster, and gardens glimpsed through wrought-iron gates is particular to this locale. But what makes it so distinct from other antique cities around the globe? Certainly, there are individual features that can be compared with corresponding things elsewhere—a Georgian Palladian portico, a Federal fanlight, faded pastel plaster like that of the Caribbean, but Charleston looks like neither Bath nor Boston, nor even Bermuda. The reality is that its streets, architecture, interiors, and gardens speak a language all their own, marrying elements from many times and places to define a stylistic dialect specific to its unique history and character.

Established in the late seventeenth century at the base of a peninsula bound by the Ashley and Cooper Rivers and the Atlantic Ocean, early Charleston looked eastward across that sea to England, not only for trade but also for design direction. Its first settlers were English and its original city plan of large blocks and broad streets, the Grand Modell, was designed to form an orderly grid. Early housing was of the primitive colonial type, but as Charleston's wealth and stability increased in the mid-eighteenth century, so did the stylistic sophistication of its residents. By the mid-1700s, some of America's finest examples of Georgian architecture were constructed here, reflecting the transmission of

OPPOSITE: The William Gibbes House, built in 1772 by a wealthy merchant-planter, is a classic Georgian double house. Its symmetry, denticulated pediment and portico, and window cornices reflect the influence of Palladian architecture on England and its colonies.

England's prevailing building aesthetic to the soil of the South. Built for successful colonists who traveled with some frequency to England and were well aware of the fine country mansions and town houses their peers were constructing, these houses were nearly as stately and refined.

Thanks to a host of English-trained artisans specializing in architectural design, wood carving, carpentry, and other skills, these dwellings reflect the close ties between Charleston's residents and their ancestral home. Books also transported the styles of England overseas, whether through volumes with etchings of ancient Greek and Roman ruins, treatises on the subject of architecture, or style manuals with detailed drawings of specific architectural details. Such books were common in gentlemen's libraries as well as at the Charleston Library Society, founded in 1748 as a subscription library for the city's elite. More than forty such books were available from local booksellers by 1772 and study of them today offers clues into design inspiration for the city's great houses and plantations.

English architects were enamored of the classical architecture of Greek and Rome throughout the eighteenth century and passed this love on to American expatriates. During the decades of that century, massive Georgian manor houses directly quoting the villas of Italian architect Andrea Palladio (1508–1580) were built in the countryside, and town houses with Palladian porticoes lined city streets. Palladio also looked to the past, quoting what was for him the familiar language of Roman architecture in his translation of temple and civic forms for private living. A new generation of architects led by Robert Adam (1728–1792) in the latter part of the eighteenth century revisited Palladio's sources as well as the architecture and wall paintings of Pompeii, excavated in 1748, to devise a new kind of neoclassicism that was more delicate, graceful, and fluid than handsome Georgian forms. Already popular in England, this style, called Adamesque there, gained favor in Charleston and other American cities around the turn of the century, becoming known as the Federal style.

Many of the individual houses fronting the streets of Charleston resemble residences across the Atlantic or above the Mason-Dixon Line, but something about the way these buildings are integrated into the streetscape seems unmistakably of this place. On a single block, you may see fine Georgian and Federal edifices next to smaller dwellings where only a hint of classical style combines with vernacular form. The vernacular form most associated with Charleston is the single house—a one-room-deep building turning its narrow end to the street and facing a side yard or carriage drive with a long porch, known locally as a piazza. These single houses may be simple wood-frame dwellings with turned spindles on their piazzas or massive masonry houses with columns in Doric, Ionic, or Corinthian orders. A row of the latter aligned along East Bay Street is a magnificent sight, but a narrow lane of diminutive wood or stuccoed houses interspersed with fragrant gardens equally beguiles.

Charleston's unique appearance can be chalked up in some ways to the law of unintended consequences. Colonial architecture is often a reductive and even naive expression of the architecture of the mother country—and this is what lends the vernacular so much charm. In Charleston, ambitious colonists fantasized about becoming New World aristocrats and dreamed of the formal architecture of England, and real estate speculators quickly constructed simple homes and tenements. In places, one can almost sense the haste of throwing up "boomtown" houses that precluded elaborate and time-consuming ornamentation. Often, the craftsmen and architects of these were not as skilled as those who had apprenticed across the Atlantic. Producing colonial interpretations of neoclassical style, they still contributed something to the streetscape that is alluring and sometimes even more memorable than the finer residences.

The city was originally planned with only a few very large, very deep lots that were quickly subdivided and divided again and interlaced with streets and alleys. This, too, contributes to Charleston's individual character, in part explaining the sideways alignment of the houses to allow for extensive rear dependencies including slave quarters, kitchens, laundries, carriage houses, and kitchen and pleasure gardens. The practice of siting houses to a slight off angle to the street in order to provide more opportune access to the prevailing breezes adds another degree of happenstance to the plan. In such a crowded urban environment, people valued privacy, which explains the presence of street-side doors that protect the piazzas from passersby, turning them into semiprivate spaces.

With so many dwellings, often constructed of wood, built in such proximity, destructive fires were an inevitable curse and they raged through town with alarming regularity, consuming scores of residences within days. The resultant gaps in the streetscape were filled, sometimes with an entire block of residences constructed in a single style and other times, with older and newer homes in varying aesthetics standing side by side. Tropical storms, earthquakes, and wartime bombardment tore through the city as well, ripping off roofs and porches, punching holes in walls, and causing some houses to list noticeably at an angle. When the sun shone, it bore down hard on the buildings, baking paint and

ABOVE: The architectural restraint of the Heyward-Washington House shows off to advantage a collection of eighteenth- and early nineteenth-century furniture, including this Queen Anne chair with ball-and-claw feet and gilded late seventeenth-century English mirror.

fading plaster to lend the city an overall patina remarked upon even in eighteenth-century accounts by visitors who described it as part of the city's exotic, romantic atmosphere, along with the fragrant gardens that grew with unruly profusion in this semitropical climate.

Climate helped shape the particular graces of the Charleston interior. A house's merit was measured not only by its architectural beauty but also its ability to provide a degree of comfort in a hot climate. High ceilings, soaring stair halls, triple-sash windows or Dutch doors opening to spacious porches, solid and louvered shutters, curved bays offering access to breezes from three directions—all these architectural responses to climate form part of Charleston's architectural appeal. The piazza was designed to protect the interior by sheltering it from light and rain and to enhance the circulation of fresh air. But despite attempts at mitigation, strong sun and humidity still had their effect within, fading textiles and damaging finishes. The Charleston summertime practice of replacing fine rugs with grass ones and draping furniture with plain white coverings was one way citizens coped with seasonal extremes.

Today, all these factors—the Anglo-classical roots of its architecture, the vernacular nature of its expression, the haphazard growth of a colonial city and evolution of its streetscape, the happenstance of fire, weather, and war, particularly the decimating effect of the Civil War that brought Charleston to its knees—inform a particular expression of Southern style. And while Charleston's style is unique, it is also archetypal for the South. Charleston today, with its blend of the old with the new, the formal with the comfortable, tradition with innovation, continues to intrigue and inspire. It is a place that has simultaneously been shaped by history and survived it, arising like a phoenix again and again from tragedy and always finding beauty and grace. Infused with passion for life, reverence for beauty, and respect for human comfort and delight, the city's architecture, rooms, and gardens offer manifold lessons that are as modern as they are antique.

RIGHT: In the withdrawing room of the Nathaniel Russell House, built in 1808, the gilded details of window surrounds and elaborate cornice decoration draw the eye upward.

The
LEXICON

The terminology of the written and spoken word is beautifully apt and even enlightening when used to discuss architecture and design. A lexicon refers to the vocabulary of an individual tongue or branch of knowledge. This assemblage of words is made of elements with specific origins—or etymology—which may be derived from earlier tongues such as Greek, Latin, French, Anglo-Saxon, and so on. In the field of design, words might be likened to a color with English origin, such as Adam blue; a classically inspired piece of furniture, such as a klismos chair; or a length of chintz with Eastern patterning. A phrase is a short group of words used together to express a particular meaning. In architecture, this could be a portico made of columns and capitals, a door crowned by a fanlight, or a compound cornice adorned with dentils and a frieze. Syntax refers to the arrangement of such words and phrases to create a well-formed sentence—a house, a room, a garden—as well as a set of rules for a certain language, as in the orders of classical architecture. Once a vocabulary has been mastered and the guides for using it understood, then the opportunities to express ideas and feelings and to describe and even shape the world are endless.

Charleston possesses a unique style lexicon, the words, phrases, and syntax of which inform streetscapes, buildings, gardens, and rooms unlike any other. The city's particular manner of communication, far from a dead language that ceased to be spoken at a certain point in time, traces an unbroken thread from the late seventeenth century to the present, its lessons many layered and far reaching. Because this mode of expression is so versatile and appealing, it continues to find exponents in and beyond the South. Thanks to the beauty and strength of its buildings, the ardor of a century-long preservation movement, and the versatility of its classical and vernacular forms, Charleston speaks a vibrant, living language both within and well beyond the city's original walls.

COLOR

In Charleston's historic district, houses with walls in shades of rose, green, yellow, and gold greet the eye, washed by the sun and tinted by the patina of centuries. Colorful shutters in contrasting shades further enliven the streetscape. These juxtapose with the subtler palette of white-painted clapboard houses with doors and shutters in Charleston green—a shade nearly indistinguishable from black. Behind the doors of restored Georgian and Federal houses, brilliant hues of aqua, apricot, cerulean, and red recall the exuberant taste of the city's eighteenth- and nineteenth-century citizens.

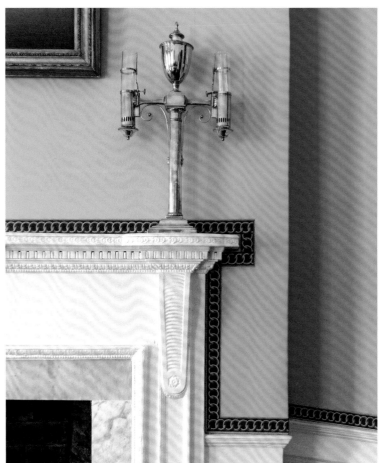

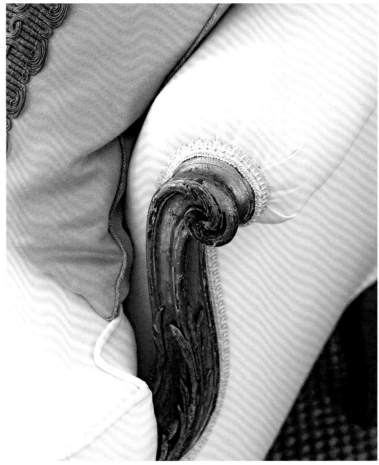

RIGHT: Scarlet upholstery and black-and-gold japanning accentuate the bold yet graceful form of an early nineteenth-century sofa in the drawing room of the Federal-period Joseph Manigault House.

OPPOSITE: A palette of verditer blue and red enlivens the dining room of the Nathaniel Russell House. Elaborate passementerie and wallpaper trim inspired by the interlocking rings of a set of chairs original to the house further animate the room's decor.

RIGHT: Historic textiles expert Natalie Larson selected the drapery and upholstery for the main bedroom of the Nathaniel Russell House. Lending the room a classical air, wallpaper trim in a Greek key pattern accents ocher-colored paint reminiscent of walls in an antique Palladian villa. Blue-and-white textiles reflecting Asian influences cool the warm color scheme.

OPPOSITE AND LEFT:
Stucco facades in a
palette of pastel tones
offer colorful contrast
to Charleston's brick,
stone, and clapboard
edifices. Contributing
a Caribbean air to
the cityscape, the
irregularities of their
sun-faded surfaces
enhance the charm
of Charleston's streets.

CRAFT

There is a kind of alchemy evident on every block of downtown Charleston, where the raw materials of clay, stone, iron, and wood have been transformed into precise and beautiful shapes. The work of many hands, including English-trained craftsmen and skilled, enslaved Africans, assembled brick walls with masonry finials, dressed and laid heavy masonry blocks, forged iron railings and gates over hot fires, and carved intricate classical motifs that crown doorways and embellish rooms. Their mastery is all the more impressive considering the primitive tools with which they worked.

RIGHT: Charleston's craftsmanship can assume weighty proportions, as seen in a brick and masonry wall accompanied by an iron gate and fence with substantial volutes and an expanse of iron balls along the base.

OPPOSITE: On the facade of a Georgian edifice, delicate ironwork and windows with spiderweb-like muntins contrast with the weightiness of dressed stone masonry.

RIGHT: While most of the carved wood moldings of the Miles Brewton House are robust and masculine, the details of the south parlor, where ladies conducted morning social calls, are more delicate and refined.

OPPOSITE: The mantel in the Nathanial Russell House's drawing room is a tour de force of composition work. A scene from *The Odyssey* combines with carved tassels, rosettes, and sheathes to exquisite effect.

GARDEN GATES

Wrought-iron gates through which verdant gardens can be glimpsed but not quite reached contribute to the entrancing spell that Charleston casts. Their designs are fanciful, with elaborate rosettes and scrolls, the silhouette of a lyre or a pineapple or even a sword. The gardens beyond may be overgrown with lush tropical greenery or pruned in the English style with axial paths. They may be fragranced with jasmine, bright with azaleas, or adorned with an elegant garden folly. With these filigree gates, Charlestonians share their gardens with passersby.

RIGHT: Substantial wrought iron fused with a cast-iron medallion combine in this gate to beautiful and powerful effect.

OPPOSITE: Almost transparent in its delicacy, the slender filigree of this wrought-iron gate forms a graceful screen through which a lovely garden and neoclassical folly can be spied.

OPPOSITE: One of Charleston's most famous gates, the 1849 Sword Gate, features a pattern of intersecting spears and swords that offers a formidable gesture amid the decorative scrollwork.

ABOVE: At Charles Towne Landing Historic Site, the lacelike tracery of a wrought-iron gate blends into the surrounding vista of old live oak trees with moss-draped limbs.

PORCHES

It's hard to think of a Southern house without a porch, but most of Charleston's earliest houses had none. Many eighteenth-century builders came from England and northern American regions where porches were uncommon. They only later discovered that a porch was a practical necessity as well as a decorative element. With single houses oriented with their long side facing a garden or drive, the lateral facade was the logical location for what Charlestonians came to call a piazza. This orientation led to the peculiar practice of having front doors that open to porches, not interior rooms.

RIGHT: A Federal-style pediment surmounts the entrance to the piazza of this house, built in 1800. While many of Charleston's South of Broad residences are built close together, this one enjoys a double lot that is visible from the sidewalk through an iron-railed fence. In the spring, a scented cloud of wisteria delights the residents and passersby alike.

RIGHT: With its semi-round form, the side porch of this majestic masonry dwelling differs from the straight lines of neighboring piazzas. The house also boasts an atypical balcony supported by massive volutes.

OPPOSITE: Oriented to face the street, this house has more in common with the dwellings of Natchez, Mississippi, than Charleston. However, its beautiful Federal entrance is true to Charleston's architectural traditions.

DOORS

Charleston's streets abound with front doors embraced by pilasters and pediments, approached by marble stairs, sheltered beneath porticoes, or tucked beneath a monumental porch that extends across the sidewalk to embrace passersby. The unique embellishment of each door not only signifies the stylistic period of the house and social status of the residents, but also contributes a generous offering to the streetscape, enhancing it with individual detail. Interior doorways are just as significant, with the quality of their adornment marking the passage from one room's degree of formality and exclusivity to the next.

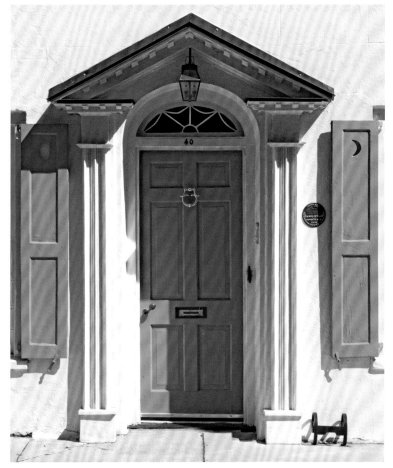

OPPOSITE: The doorways opening to Charleston piazzas frequently feature handsome classical details like this denticulated pediment.

ABOVE: Built circa 1767, this house is a rare example of a colonial side-passage plan. The front door opens to a side hall as opposed to more typical Georgian doors that lead to center halls.

LEFT: Interior doors occasionally received even greater embellishment than exterior ones, as demonstrated by the faux-flame-grain-mahogany withdrawing room doors of the Nathaniel Russell House.

47

WINDOWS

In Charleston's finest houses, windows afford views and allow natural light to enter while also issuing an invitation to embellish the facade and interior space. For eighteenth- and nineteenth-century architects, windows provided an opportunity to emulate and imaginatively reinterpret classical, English neoclassical, and Federal forms. Stately Palladian windows add grace to facades and elegant fanlights enliven doors. Inside the house, exquisitely carved moldings and gilded details transform windows into architectural tours de force. Dressed in elaborate drapery, they signal the wealth and taste of the residents.

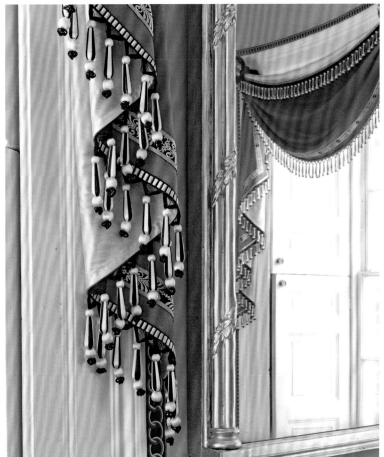

RIGHT: Generously proportioned windows framed by double pilasters and sizable gouge-work architraves bring light and air into the oval dining room of the Joseph Manigault House, built in 1803. Following the line of the room's curve, the architectonic surrounds of the windows provide robust, masculine contrast to the plaster entablature's delicate garlands and rosettes.⸙

OPPOSITE: Colorful wooden shutters that contrast with walls of tinted plaster are a typical sight in Charleston's historic district. Compared to those in Boston and Philadelphia, the city's houses have more and larger windows that provide enhanced ventilation during the long hot season.

ABOVE: The patina of shutter dogs and louvered shutters painted in a matching color add verdigris accents to the Aiken-Rhett House's tawny stucco walls.

WALLS

In Charleston's most elaborately decorated residences, a wall is rarely just a wall. It is a canvas upon which craftsmen exercised their talents and creativity to devise rooms of taste and sophistication. Marbleized wallpaper mimicked the polished stone walls a family might have observed on a Grand Tour of Italy. Paneling crowned with cornices emulated the designs of sixteenth-century Italian architect Andrea Palladio. Painted wood or plaster or a solid field of wallpaper accented by patterned trim echoed Georgian and Adamesque styles, bringing cosmopolitan flair to Charleston's walls.

OPPOSITE: Wainscoting trimmed with classical motifs was a popular wall treatment in the Federal period. At the Nathaniel Russell House, additional embellishment comes in the form of wallpaper trim with a lamb's-tongue pattern found in the room's moldings.

LEFT: Colorful faux-marbre wallpaper like this example from the Edmondston-Alston House reminded nineteenth-century Charlestonians who enjoyed traveling abroad of the marble walls they admired in Italy.

STAIRS

Charleston abounds in beautiful stairs that are often the first thing to greet the eye upon entering a home. Making a strong first impression, they also offer an invitation to ascend to entertaining rooms on the second floor. Two of the finest Federal curved stairs in Charleston wind upward through the halls of the Nathaniel Russell and Joseph Manigault houses toward exquisitely detailed drawing and withdrawing rooms. At Drayton Hall, a Georgian split staircase, originally painted eye-catching vermilion, led to the grandest room in an already grand country house.

LEFT: The south entrance of the Joseph Manigault House offers a dramatic view in which a wide arch frames the soaring silhouette of a stair winding upward to the second floor. The stair follows the curve of an elliptical bay possessing double doors that open on the northern facade and once served as the carriage entrance. A generously proportioned Palladian window illuminates the composition.

61

RIGHT: In a guesthouse constructed of antique brick, a spiral staircase designed by Charleston architect Eddie Fava expresses the grace of a Federal stair in contemporary style and material.

OPPOSITE: In the elliptical stair hall of the Joseph Manigault House, a cornice molding featuring triglyphs and rosettes draws the eye upward toward the magnificent ceiling medallion crowning the space.

LEFT: At Drayton Hall, the handsome paneling of the stair hall and stately form of the divided stair epitomize Georgian style. A carved grapevine motif and the sinuous pattern of a carved-plaster ceiling in the landing's soffit introduce organic forms into the geometric space. With most of the paneling originally painted yellow ocher and the wainscoting, mahogany handrails, balusters, and decorative brackets, vermilion, the stair hall's original impact was even more powerful than it is today.

MANTELS

In the entertaining rooms of Charleston houses, the status of the mantel as a ceremonial object equals if not surpasses its function as a source of heat. Adorned with Italian marble, Delft tiles, fluted pilasters, carved volutes, classical motifs, or finely worked panels of composition, they become architectonic flights of fancy that add beauty to already elaborate rooms. Whether a Georgian mantel with a handsome overmantel that doubles its impact or an elegantly precise Federal one, their gesture is one of welcome and their invitation is to gather around.

ABOVE: Original paneling and moldings in the dining room of the 1743 George Eveleigh House include this simple Georgian bolection molding encasing the fireplace.

OPPOSITE: The mantel and overmantel of the Heyward-Washington House's drawing room combines classical elements including volutes and pilasters with baroque-style relief featuring a figure-eight pattern popular in eighteenth-century Charleston.

OPPOSITE: Delft tiles faithfully reproducing the original eighteenth-century ones decorate the drawing room mantel at the Miles Brewton House. Their maritime motifs refer to Brewton's profession as a merchant.

LEFT: A pearl molding employed throughout the drawing room of the Edmondston-Alston House, built circa 1825, softens the more severe, rectilinear shapes of the mantel, door, and window surrounds.

ABOVE: Although the mantel of Drayton Hall's drawing room was stolen by vandals, the robust overmantel survives along with the room's highly embellished moldings and carved-in-place plaster ceiling.

OPPOSITE: In contrast with the Georgian ornamentation of Drayton Hall, the later, neoclassical details of the Nathaniel Russell House dining room are more delicate in scale and decoration.

ANTIQUES

Colonial Charleston was a place that valued fashion. As soon as its planters, merchants, and traders of various goods attained sufficient wealth, they ordered au courant furniture from abroad, particularly England, that allowed them to live in luxurious style. Before long, the city's joiners and cabinetmakers, many trained in Europe, began making equally refined pieces, often copied from popular style books like Thomas Chippendale's *The Gentleman and Cabinet-Maker's Director*. In the post–Civil War era, impoverished Charlestonians clung to their heirlooms or sold them when necessary, refashioning the city as a mecca for antiques.

RIGHT: A circa 1750 chest-on-chest secretary displays exquisite marquetry with an arched Palladian motif and recessed shell design.

OPPOSITE, UPPER LEFT: A Charleston-made breakfast table in the Heyward-Washington House possesses meticulously carved open fretwork on its end panels. UPPER RIGHT: Eighteenth-century Italian chairs bring fluid lines into the stately setting of the Miles Brewton House. LOWER LEFT: The gilt-wood frame of a late nineteenth-century French looking glass demonstrates interior designer Alexandra Howard's passion for the patina of old gold. LOWER RIGHT: An eighteenth-century linen press in the Heyward-Washington House boasts exquisite carved mahogany fretwork and realistic rosettes.

OPPOSITE: With straight legs and a pierced splat, this chair in the collection of the Heyward-Washington House is a classic expression of the Chippendale style.

LEFT: A monumental library bookcase, also in the Heyward-Washington House, was made circa 1800 in the shop of Charleston cabinetmaker Robert Walker. It displays masterful craftsmanship with its bookmarked wood grain, intricate marquetry, and slender muntins.

CHINA, CRYSTAL, SILVER

The dressing of the table, sideboard, and mantel are high arts of ceremonial import in the Charleston home. As if making offerings to the muses of hospitality and home, Charlestonians arrange finely wrought objects from afar around their rooms to reflect sunlight, glitter in candlelight, and lend color to dark mahogany furnishings. Planters and merchants commissioned silver from London and hand-painted porcelain from China or France to set tables where cut glass and etched crystal brought diamond-like brilliance. Enhancing the beauty of their surroundings, these precious, fragile objects became the jewelry of the house.

OPPOSITE: A mirrored Italian bowfront server, circa 1800, proves the perfect place to display an elegant English tea service and figured porcelain urn.

ABOVE: The antique meets the modern in this composition of heirloom silver and eighteenth-century export porcelain arranged on an acrylic table.

The
HOUSES
&
GARDENS

MIDDLETON PLACE

WHEN IT COMES to the garden lexicon of Charleston and the surrounding Low Country, the garden at Middleton Place has it all, from a thousand-year-old live oak tree to tender jessamine blossoms, geometric boxwood parterres, mounds and allées of azaleas, Italian marble statuary, and cypress stumps. Neoclassically inspired and New World sited, the garden brings together the intellectual rigor of eighteenth-century French landscape architecture with the irrepressible semitropical flora of the American South, resulting in an incomparable masterpiece of landscape design. Given that it is harder to protect gardens than houses from the long-term effects of time, as some plants grow wild while others die, the pristine character of this man-made landscape today represents a miracle of preservation.

The originators of the garden, the plan of which dates to 1741, include an unknown English landscape architect whose work captures the elegance and rationality of the gardens of André Le Nôtre as demonstrated at Versailles and Vaux-le-Vicomte. This choice of style reflects the sophistication of the plantation's first Middleton owner, Henry Middleton, who acquired the property through marriage. Henry Middleton grew up in a well-to-do British colonial society that valued worldly things, classical education, and travel across the seas. He would have been aware of the architectural and landscape fashions in vogue on

the far side of the Atlantic and eager to emulate them on his own rice plantation as a sign of his wealth, refinement, and membership in an elite, global aristocracy.

Such French-style formal gardens already flourished around grand English country houses, which made sense considering the proximity and similarities in climate of England and France. But the re-creation of the strict axial geometries of the French neoclassical garden amid the unruly profusion of South Carolina's semitropical flora, primeval forest, and marshy riverbanks offers a study in contrasts that would have surely surprised and delighted visitors from abroad. The plan for the original garden possesses logical, isosceles order, superimposing upon the natural landscape a triangle of axes, one which parallels the Ashley River. The second travels toward the now-ruined plantation house, continuing to bisect a terraced lawn, while the third defines a long canal afloat with swans.

The creation of this garden involved the work of more than a hundred enslaved Africans who worked for ten years to realize the plan. Slave labor also supported the garden's ongoing development by subsequent generations of Middletons, as well as the surrounding rice plantation's operations. The garden continued to grow under the watch of Henry's grandson, also named Henry Middleton, who embellished the landscape plan in the late eighteenth and early nineteenth centuries. At a time when natural sciences were considered an important part of a gentleman's education, Henry acquired an interest in botany. Through a friendship with French botanist Henri Michaux, who was experimenting with flora in the Low Country, Henry planted some of the first *Camellia japonica* in America, introducing what would become a staple of Southern garden design. Henry's son,

Williams, became fascinated with the azalea, the brilliantly hued bush now widely associated with springtime in the South. This Middleton extended the reach of the garden to include a mound of multicolored azaleas that reflects in the rice millpond visible from the house. In keeping with the aesthetics of the nineteenth-century English romantic movement, he also incorporated a wilderness cypress garden.

Following the Civil War, the garden fell into ruin, melting back into the semitropical landscape. Fifty years after the war, Boston poet Amy Lowell described it as "sad as a tomb." But new generations of the family revived it, led by Mrs. J. J. Pringle Smith, who inherited the property in 1915. Gradually reclaiming order out of chaos, Smith was awarded a prestigious medal by the Garden Club of America in 1941. Later that century, her son, Charles Duell, furthered the restoration and expanded Middleton Place's reach by supervising the estate's transition from a family owned property to a not-for-profit open to the public. While the many enslaved Africans who aided in the garden's creation in the eighteenth and nineteenth centuries lacked surnames, it's impossible to talk of the landscape without crediting them: Emanuel, Bob, Winter, Anthony, Willoughby, Priscilla, Louisa, and Andrewina, among unnamed others. Attesting to the generations of white and black, free and enslaved people who created and maintained it, Middleton Place continues to delight and surprise visitors today.

PREVIOUS PAGE: The main house at Middleton Place plantation, built circa 1705, burned in the Civil War, but this flanker with romantic Flemish-style gables, built in 1755, remains.

OPPOSITE: The mill, constructed in the mid-eighteenth century, served as both a place to mill rice and a romantic garden folly visible from the house.

RIGHT: The garden at Middleton Place was inspired by the design principles of André Le Nôtre, landscape architect for Louis XIV's Versailles, for whom rational, geometric order was paramount. The canal defines one of the lines of a triangular arrangement of axes that shaped the design of the original garden.

RIGHT: Middleton Place is famous for its camellias, which thanks to the second Henry Middleton's friendship with emigrant French botanist Henri Michaux, include the first four to be planted in an American garden.

OPPOSITE: Standing in a circle of hydrangeas, the marble figure of a sandal binder, circa 1819, is among the few survivors of family-owned statues, most of which were destroyed in the Civil War.

PAGES 94 AND 95: The octagonal sunken garden outlined by boxwood parterres is laid out in a geometrically precise position that conforms to the triangular system of axes central to the garden plan.

OPPOSITE AND LEFT: Eliza's House, built in 1870 as home to African-American plantation workers, demonstrates the living conditions of families during that era.

DRAYTON HALL

SITTING LIKE A sphinx on the edge of the Ashley River, Drayton Hall is a majestic presence full of history, mystery, and evidence of life in what seems a distant age. Because each wall of painted cypress, every carefully formed plaster ceiling, and the meticulously carved moldings and mantels are touched only lightly by modern hands, the house feels alive. It speaks for itself to those who listen, silently telling the stories of the seven generations of the Drayton family who owned it and the enslaved and free African Americans who lived and worked in the house from its eighteenth-century construction to its twentieth-century sale to the National Trust for Historic Preservation. Despite the passage of three centuries, the vicissitudes of war, and the power of semi-tropical storms, it stands nearly unchanged by time. From the presence of its ceiling medallions and wood cornices to the absence of modern amenities such as electricity and plumbing, the house is carefully guarded by the Trust, whose philosophy toward the property is one of preservation rather than restoration.

Historians have long sifted through documents trying to determine the architect of this dwelling, the earliest and finest example of Palladian architecture in colonial America. New research suggests that the house, built between 1738 and 1752, was designed by John Drayton himself, a second-generation South Carolinian who grew up on the adjacent Magnolia Plantation.

A prosperous planter and active member of British colonial government most likely educated in England, Drayton turned to his mother country for inspiration when building his colonial dwelling. There, architects had turned to ancient Greece and Rome for insight and to the villas designed by sixteenth-century Italian architect Andrea Palladio. Young Drayton probably visited the Palladian manor houses his English peers were constructing in the countryside during the eighteenth century and was likely fascinated by the subject. His library is believed to have included multiple volumes on classical and contemporaneous architecture, some featuring details that make an appearance in Drayton Hall.

Order and hierarchy reigns throughout Palladian design, from the literal order of the columns from Doric to Corinthian to the symmetry of rooms that progress from the plainest, intended for conducting business, to the most extravagantly ornamented drawing rooms. Such architecture sought to convey a message of wealth and political dominion and reinforced class distinctions. At Drayton Hall, the cellar, or in Palladio's terms, *baso*, was designated for living and working spaces for the enslaved Africans who made the Draytons' luxurious lifestyle possible. Its rough brick and white-washed walls coexist in stark contrast with the refined details of the upper floors. Whereas the windows and doors of the upper levels were designed for maximum ventilation and personal comfort, the basement's windows are small and doors were often sealed to keep cooking smells from traveling upstairs.

Drayton Hall was intended as a place to entertain as well as one in which to live. Dressed to impress, it greeted visitors who approached by carriage with a majestic two-story portico rising between two flankers and connecting colonnades. A traditional English landscape with a strong central axis amid which trees and gardens were arranged in irregular fashion reinforced the grandeur of the scene. A more private garden overlooking the river, designed to be enjoyed by the most highly valued guests, lay on the far side of the house. A grand stair hall with vermilion-colored painted paneling faces this garden, climbing to the most exclusive and highly decorated rooms of the house. Time has gradually changed or faded the original colors of the house but has done little to dull the detail of the adjacent great hall's neoclassical rosette, triglyph, and egg-and-dart moldings or the drawing room's Ionic pilasters and carved-in-place plaster ceiling.

History has brushed this dwelling, with destruction wrought by the Revolutionary and Civil Wars, as well as the late nineteenth-century mining of phosphates on the property and demolition of the flankers at the turn of the nineteenth century. During the Great Depression, despite the house's lack of electricity, indoor plumbing, or modern kitchen, Drayton descendants used it as a summer retreat in what can only be imagined as a kind of architectural glamping. Throughout these challenges and circumstances, the Drayton family remained steadfast in its dedication to protecting the history of the property, preserving this remarkable structure as the tangible remains of many varied times and lives gone by.

PREVIOUS PAGE: Constructed of handmade bricks and monumental limestone columns in the mid-eighteenth century by enslaved Africans, Drayton Hall's impressive edifice features an unusual portico. The first of its kind in the world, the two-story portico simultaneously projects from and recedes into the facade.

OPPOSITE: Details of the great hall's hand-carved wood moldings can be traced to contemporaneous volumes concerning Georgian and classical design that likely inspired their makers.

RIGHT: From the floral-inspired mahogany swags above the windows to the architectonic cypress-wood details of the paneling and mantel, the drawing room's hand-carved elements demonstrate the expertise of early South Carolina craftsmen, most of whom learned their craft in England. A rare carved-in-place plaster ceiling reveals both skill and a touch of naivete in its execution.

OPPOSITE AND ABOVE: While the divided staircase of Drayton Hall expresses the qualities of harmonious geometry and symmetry prized by Georgian architects, the decorative plaster ceiling and window decorations of the drawing room point to the curvilinear natural forms also celebrated in English and French baroque design.

RIGHT: In the basement where enslaved African Americans toiled to support the luxury of Drayton Hall's upper floors, pine plank doors and brick floors were considered sufficient.

OPPOSITE: In 1815, Charles Drayton replaced damaged first-floor columns with limestone copies, leaving a pile of columns and capitals in the basement.

106

MILES BREWTON HOUSE

LIVES COME AND they pass. Fortunes rise and they fall. But sometimes a monument remains that tells their stories — a *memento mori* and, in the case of the Miles Brewton House, a *memento vivere* as well. Built for Miles Brewton, circa 1769, on a double lot on King Street, this dwelling is now home to his eighth- and ninth-generation descendants who actively preserve it and keep its history alive. When Brewton commissioned Charleston's best London-trained contractor and artisans to build the mansion, his fortunes were rising on the tide of Charleston's thriving economy. Like his peers in the city's merchant and planter elite, he desired a residence in keeping with the finest English architecture and furnished in similar style.

By that time, Charleston had a growing population of carpenters, joiners, carvers, and contractors who, having learned their trade in England, immigrated to South Carolina. The city was also awash in publications on the subject, including more than twenty books in the collection of the Charleston Library Society, of which Brewton was a member. Ezra Waite, who was responsible for much of the house's design and carving, owned several volumes and employed designs from them. Like the best in his trade, his artistry featured interpretation and originality in combining elements into unique designs. Waite was one among many craftsmen employed by the building's contractor, Richard

Moncrieff, recognized as one of Charleston's best. This team created a monumental facade dominated by a two-story portico quoting the designs of sixteenth-century Italian architect Andrea Palladio, whose villas inspired Georgian design on both sides of the Atlantic. Within, a typical Georgian center-hall, four-room plan divides the ground floor into a series of chambers including two highly embellished parlors.

Mr. and Mrs. Peter Manigault, eighth-generation owners of the house, undertook a comprehensive restoration project from 1988 to 1991, employing scholars who studied every aspect of the house's design. Among discoveries was the use of papier-mâché appliqué decoration in lieu of plaster in several rooms, including on the south parlor's ceiling, which features garlands and birds. This lends a light touch, as does the scale and detail of this room's carvings, which are more delicately proportioned than elsewhere in the house. The parlor's furnishings are equally refined, including a set of eighteenth-century Italian chairs acquired when a member of the family served in an ambassadorial capacity in Venice. With stately dentils and a broken-architrave overmantel, the north parlor, used today as a dining room, is more masculine in appearance. Here, the occupants display heirlooms that would have originally graced the room, including silver by master English silversmith Matthew Boulton and Chinese porcelain. Among these pieces is a trophy that one of the more colorful former residents, Colonel William Alston, commissioned in England after his horse won a Charleston race. Apparently, none was on offer at the racecourse.

The finest chamber is the twenty-seven by twenty-foot drawing room on the second floor, which spans the front of the house and opens to the portico. In 1773, Joseph Quincy of Boston described it as "[t]he grandest hall I ever beheld, azure blue satin window curtains, rich blue paper with gilt, mashee borders, most elegant pictures, excessive grand and costly looking glasses, etc." Today, the room seems no less extravagant, thanks to the restoration of its azure ceiling as well as the blue upholstery on an original set of eighteenth-century chairs with damask woven on Prelle looms in Lyon, France. A reproduction of the original gilded papier-mâché fillet, copied from a fragment found in a rat's nest behind a carved molding, draws the eye above the handsomely detailed cornices and door surrounds to the high ceiling.

Tiny fragments also informed the restoration of other rooms, including the library, where wallpaper is trimmed with a brilliant orange anthemia motif, and the main bedroom, where a bold blue-and-white print creates a dramatic effect. While the thoroughness of this restoration is thanks to Mr. and Mrs. Manigault, the building's preservation can also be attributed to the Frost sisters who resided there in the early twentieth century, including Susan Pringle Frost, founder of Charleston's preservation movement. Over the years the house has seen tragedy—Miles Brewton and his family were lost at sea and descendants sacrificed lives and fortunes in the Civil War—but today's current resident, Lee Manigault, has perpetuated the house's spirit of conviviality in a recent book of Charleston etiquette and recipes. Another line of Latin sums up the message of the house—*ars longa, vita brevis.*

PREVIOUS PAGE: Declared a National Historic Landmark, the Miles Brewton House features a classical portico with columns in the Doric and Ionic orders.

OPPOSITE: The library's walls are embellished with faithfully reproduced verditer blue wallpaper decorated with contrasting patterned trim.

RIGHT: The drawing room of the Miles Brewton House is one of the most exquisitely crafted Georgian rooms in America. In this chamber, restrained window surrounds allow the elaborately detailed cornice and ceiling to dominate the design. Gilt fillets draw the eye upward toward the apex of the vaulted ceiling where a coved molding offers more opportunity for intricate carved-wood decoration.

RIGHT: In the south parlor where the ladies of the house received morning calls, papier-mâché ceiling ornamentation with a bird motif produces an airy, lacelike impression. The carved wood decoration of the window surrounds and cornice are equally delicate in their design.

OPPOSITE: The master bedroom's wallpaper, which features a variation of the Prince of Wales feather motif, was reproduced from an original piece discovered sealing the horsehair stuffing of the drawing room's chairs.

NATHANIEL RUSSELL HOUSE

IF VISITORS TODAY were unaware that in the intervening centuries this dwelling had been inhabited by multiple families, a female academy, and a convent school, they might easily assume that the year was 1808 and that its original owners, Mr. and Mrs. Russell, had just stepped out for a walk. Nearly everything about the house, from the brilliant colors of the walls to the polish of antique furnishings, projects a pristine image of the early nineteenth-century lifestyle of Charleston's fashionable elite. But by the early twentieth century, the building and its extensive grounds were endangered. Threatened with the prospect of modern encroachment, the property was purchased in 1955 through Historic Charleston Foundation's newly created revolving fund, marking an important turning point in the city's preservation movement. Since then, the Nathaniel Russell House, considered one of the finest Federal dwellings in America, has become a model of historic restoration with meticulous research and scientific analysis revealing insights into its original appearance and the lives and minds of those who created and inhabited it.

Like a time capsule within a time capsule, the details of the house hold evidence of even earlier times, bringing to life the millennium and more of the architectural and design influences that shaped it. Within this fabric, countless artifacts point to historic times—ancient Greece and Rome, the Italian

Renaissance, the Gothic period, and eighteenth-century England's neoclassical phases of architecture. Handsome architrave windows, Corinthian and Ionic mantelpieces, Greek key and lamb's-tongue wallpaper trim, cornices abounding in classical detail, a decorative panel depicting a scene from the Odyssey—these all speak of the architecture of ancient Greece and Rome. They also point to Italian Renaissance architect Andrea Palladio, who repurposed these forms and motifs in noble Italian villas and to the British Georgian architects who quoted Palladio, applying his ideas to early eighteenth-century country houses. The delicate intricacy of the house's details corresponds to the later wave of neoclassical design spearheaded by Scottish architect Robert Adam, father of the Adamesque aesthetic that inspired America's Federal style.

When Nathaniel Russell spent two years in London in the early 1780s, evading the chaos of Revolutionary War–era Charleston, the Adamesque movement was the height of fashion. He surely visited town houses and estates designed in the style and would have been impressed. Like many members of Charleston's planter and mercantile class, Russell yearned for an American residence that would equal those of the British aristocracy. There is no known architect for the house he built—its design may well have been directed by Russell himself—but its form and details directly quote elements of the grand English town houses with which he was familiar. It is also replete with decorative flourishes that appeared in architectural pattern books published in England and widely consulted on this side of the Atlantic. Many of the antique forms, from the dentils and egg and darts of the drawing room's cornice molding and the columns of the mantelpieces, can be found in these volumes.

These elements, however, are employed with originality, including a layer of Gothic detail amid the drawing room's classical cornice. A figure-eight design popular in Charleston's baroque era finds its place, carved into moldings and door surrounds. The drawing room's oval shape and forced symmetry, with curved and mirrored wall panels balancing corresponding windows across the room, directly quote Adamesque conceits. The fanciful faux–lapis lazuli plinths in the drawing room recall details from Pompeian wall paintings. In the adjoining drawing room, a similar melding of classical, Palladian, and neoclassical styles defines the gilded cornices, denticulated architraves, and slender fluted pilasters. The strong colors of the house also reference historical aesthetics, with the dining room's Adam blue walls and the bedroom's ocher paint that calls to mind the aged plaster walls of old Italian villas. Taken as a whole, the complex design lexicon of the Russell House communicates two messages: the global sophistication of Charleston's eighteenth- and nineteenth-century residents and the deep history that inspired the timeless beauty of the rooms they made.

PREVIOUS PAGE: While the facade of the Nathaniel Russell House, constructed in 1808, demonstrates the Federal era's emphasis on symmetry, the side bay accommodating an elliptical dining room demonstrates the influence of English architect Robert Adam, who also favored asymmetrical room arrangements.

OPPOSITE: A door with intricately composed muntins surmounted by a fanlight separates the vestibule, which was the most public space in the house, from the private domain. Its glass panes allow light to travel from the vestibule's windows into the stair hall.

PREVIOUS SPREAD:
The oval drawing room expresses the full range of decorative detail popular in the English Adamesque and American Federal movements, including the architectonic Palladian forms of the window surrounds, curvilinear baroque motifs, and the less common Gothic Revival tracery of the cornice. The room's brilliant coloration is based on expert paint analysis.

RIGHT: A curvaceous recamier sofa with sapphire blue upholstery and gilded florets enhances its elegant setting.

OPPOSITE: The mantelpiece features delicate fluted columns and a composition-work scene from *The Odyssey*.

LEFT: Forensic research determined that the dining room once featured wallpaper with a solid verditer blue field, re-created during the recent restoration. Period-appropriate trim featuring an interlocking ring motif was also applied during the restoration. Charleston-made furniture in the room includes a circa 1880 sideboard and Pembroke table.

AIKEN-RHETT HOUSE

JUST AS THE Rosetta stone offered a key for deciphering the hitherto inscrutable language of Egyptian hieroglyphs by presenting them in conjunction with Greek and Roman letters, the Aiken-Rhett House provides insight by juxtaposing the varied style languages of Charleston. Completed in 1820 in the Federal style by Charleston merchant John Robinson, the house was swiftly remodeled in the Greek Revival style by its second owner, William Aiken Sr., a wealthy railroad magnate. Upon his death, his son, William Aiken Jr., later to become the governor of South Carolina, undertook another remodeling in 1858, redecorating rooms and adding an Italianate art gallery. During his residency, he expanded the slave quarters and outbuildings and embellished them with Gothic Revival features. These well-preserved structures offer yet more clues to the diverse aesthetic and social spectrum of the city's architecture.

Robinson's house possessed a typical two-over-two room form with a wide center hall, embellished throughout with the delicate neoclassicism associated with the Federal period. Although evidence of this original style has been erased from the entertaining rooms, remnants can still be found in the bedrooms and most dramatically, on the ceiling of the stair hall where a magnificent fluted plaster medallion floats many feet above the landing. The gossamer quality of this embellishment diverges from the robustly ornate Greek Revival

medallions found in the double parlors, as well as the dining room and drawing room added in the 1830s.

The decoration of these rooms expresses the bold, at times brash, attitudes of the South's antebellum elite who experienced great wealth and dominion over a region owing much of its economic success to an enslaved labor system. Monumental cornice moldings and door and window surrounds dominate the rooms for entertainment where lavishly detailed ceiling medallions would have dazzled in the glimmering light of chandeliers. These were set off by walls painted Pompeian blue, a shade familiar to well-traveled Southerners and Europeans whose extended tours of Italy often included the ancient city. In an account written by Swedish author Fredrika Bremer of her 1850 visit to Charleston, she describes an event in this room. "There was very beautiful music; and . . . conversation in the room, or out under the piazzas . . . . Five hundred persons, it is said, were invited, and the entertainment was one of the most beautiful I have been present at in this country."

Soon after this party, the second generation of Aikens to inhabit the house redecorated the room, introducing a French accent with panels of wallpaper, likely purchased on a trip to France, framed by gilded moldings. The walls were repainted pink to accentuate the colorful flourishes of the wallpaper's pattern. Further embellishment came in the form of wallpaper trim with motifs that resemble both Gothic and Moorish prototypes. Combined with marble mantels from Italy, iron sconces with Turkish-style crescent moons, and the plethora of classical detail, the effect reveals the global quality of the residents' sensibility and lifestyle.

This kind of worldliness was as much a social statement as an aesthetic one. Travel abroad and the collecting of decorative objects and art demonstrated wealth and sophistication and heightened social status. The art gallery that Aiken Jr. added to the house in 1857 is a testament to his family's position at the fore of Charleston society. Decorated in a mélange of Italianate and Rococo Revival styles, the room houses marble sculptures and paintings including works by American expatriates in Rome and copies of Italian masterpieces purchased abroad by Aiken Jr. and his wife. Miraculously, these works of art survived the looting of the house by Union troops in 1865 and were retained by subsequent generations of the Aiken family.

Clearly visible through the windows of a library where costly volumes still fill bookcases, the slave quarters offer stark contrast. Forbidden to read or write and prevented from escaping by tall garden walls, the enslaved workers lived and toiled in cramped, dark spaces. Research indicates, however, that some of the rooms were brightly painted, including walls tinted ultramarine, an expensive blue paint likely leftover from decorating the main house. Residents and their guests would have passed within feet of these primitive rooms to reach a pleasure garden and Gothic-style folly, enjoying leisure in proximity to the people who made their way of life possible, underscoring both the intimacy and division between the two poles of the antebellum South's society.

RIGHT: Upon inheriting the house, William Aiken Jr. and his wife, Harriet, swiftly enlarged it, attaching a two-story addition including a drawing room with walls once covered with gold- and silver-trimmed crimson flocked wallpaper. After Aiken died, Harriet turned the extravagantly decorated chamber into her bedroom.

RIGHT: In the slave quarters, sleeping rooms possessed small interior windows allowing light and air to filter in through the hall. The narrow passage's windows overlook a walled work area and garden.

OPPOSITE: At Christmastime, the table in the Aiken-Rhett House dining room is still dressed with china, crystal, and silver that was utilized by previous residents.

ANDREW & JULIE GOULD HOUSE

MUCH OF THE charm of Charleston's streetscape comes from its irregularity. While the area of the original city was first divided into a grid of large lots, this orderly plan quickly became tangled. Portions of lots were sold to new settlers and real estate speculators, creeks filled in and turned into lanes, and dead-end alleys carved into the cityscape. Houses were built cheek by jowl, with barely enough room for a carriage to pass between, and lush flora overreached the boundaries of garden fences to festoon the streets, establishing an intimacy between garden and street, dwelling and neighbor, inhabitant and passerby. This spirit informed Catfiddle Street, a new lane meandering through the interior of a large block of extant houses far above Broad. With buildings in proximity, private gardens blurring into shared walkways, and architecture directly quoting Palladian, Georgian, and Italianate styles, the tiny neighborhood offers a Lilliputian experience of Charleston's urban spirit.

Andrew Gould, one of the project's visionaries and an architectural design consultant, tapped the history-rooted character of the street when he created his residence in the style of Charleston's settlers' late seventeenth-century dwellings. His lot was small, so it seemed natural to build a tall, narrow house in the Dutch style with a gambrel roof characteristic of the city's first residences. With only a thousand square feet of living space inhabited by a family of five, as

PREVIOUS PAGE:
Conceived by architectural designer Andrew Gould, this present-day house combines a masonry main block with a gambrel roof reminiscent of Charleston's earliest colonial dwellings with a Georgian-style addition featuring wooden quoins and oculus windows.

RIGHT: Inspired by seventeenth-century Jacobean examples, Gould designed and crafted the main house's square-knobbed newel post and turned spindles.

was often the case in colonial dwellings, the original home ultimately required an addition, which gave Gould an opportunity to stretch his imagination. For the addition, he imagined a second- or third-generation resident expanding the existing house in the early Georgian/English baroque taste.

Wooden quoins and pedimented windows give the addition a distinct colonial Georgian appearance. Within, it contains a small yet stately dining room with sophisticated architectural details that contrast with the adjacent early-colonial-style sitting room's rustic beams and plank walls. Like the grand entertaining rooms of lower Charleston's mansions, the dining room hovers above street level, affording large double-hung windows with interior shutters that overlook the street and neighboring dwellings. A barrel-vaulted ceiling provides vertical lift, as does woodwork inspired by an overmantel at Drayton Hall, which creates a terminus at the end of the dinner table. A paint scheme with seven shades of green and gold, and walls hung with Orthodox icons, suggest a malachite-paneled hall in a Russian imperial palace—grandeur one wouldn't expect in a small room with beadboard walls.

Like the palette of the dining room, the colors of the adjoining sitting room were influenced by Renee Killian-Dawson, an interior designer based in England with special knowledge of historical paint colors. In keeping with mid-seventeenth-century design, the sitting room features a ceiling of reclaimed heart pine with a summer beam and hand-carved ogee and lamb's-tongue carving, all executed by Gould, an expert carpenter. The Jacobean-style turned spindles and newel post of the stair add dignity and graphic dynamism to the small space. The heart of the room is a plaster-over-brick fireplace complete with a bread oven–like aperture to the adjacent kitchen. Intentionally primitive, it serves as not only a welcoming hearth but also a backdrop for icons Gould and his wife, Julie, both converts to Eastern Orthodoxy, collect.

While it is unlikely that seventeenth- or eighteenth-century members of the Russian Orthodoxy were among the immigrants populating Charleston in the colonial era, this house proffers a fantasy of what such a family's dwelling might have been. In a way, much of Charleston's architecture is rooted in dreams—with titled colonists establishing New World town houses and country seats and parvenus building fancy residences to mimic those of England. Borrowing from the exalted language of Greek and Roman temples, the Palladian villas of the Veneto, and Robert Adam's lexicon, they created a charmed and charming city. The Gould residence and the new Charleston lane where it stands convey this spirit of endeavor and imagination into the modern age, demonstrating that the dream of Charleston lives on into the twenty-first century.

OPPOSITE: Intentionally archaic in material, texture, and craftsmanship, the room the residents call the library possesses a floor and ceiling of reclaimed wood, walls clad with twelve-inch-wide boards, and a stucco-over-brick wall and fireplace resembling a kitchen hearth. The opposite side of the wall faces the actual kitchen.

Limited by the allowable footprint for the addition and inspired by the long galleries of English manor houses, Gould designed an addition with a narrow, rectangular form. On the first floor, this space incorporates a single room with areas for dining at one end and sitting at the other. The barrel-vaulted ceiling and walls of cabinets accentuate the elongated shape of the room.

141

ABOVE: Openings resembling bread and warming ovens pierce the stucco-over-brick wall that divides the kitchen from the adjoining library.

OPPOSITE: Gould fashioned a strong visual focal point for the dining room with woodwork reminiscent of Drayton Hall's overmantel. The dining room's antique reproductions of primitively crafted seventeenth-century chairs relate to the colonial style of the adjacent library.

JOHNSON'S ROW

THE STORY OF the French Quarter's Johnson's Row, constructed in the late eighteenth century just above Broad Street, is one of history preserved and revived. Like many of Charleston's early dwellings, including the town houses of Rainbow Row, it was built as a tenement—or upscale rental property. At the time, the city was a burgeoning mercantile and agricultural center and real estate investors, including William Johnson of New York, saw attractive business opportunities. Part of a row of buildings originally accommodating street-front offices with residences above, the house now owned by Rick Wilson and David Trachtenberg features cypress paneling, classical moldings, carved mantelpieces, and large windows for comfort and light, with much of the material original and documented by Historic Charleston Foundation.

Visitors immediately realize the historic quality of the house upon entering and seeing the dining room, where cypress paneling, handsome in the simplicity of its detail, lines the walls. With boards of varying width, its mellow surface enwraps a Georgian mantel of similarly toned cypress. Above this hangs a portrait of Wilson's fourth-great-grandmother, Mary Mazyck, painted circa 1770 by an artist in Newport, Rhode Island. A collection of 1710 pastel portraits by Henrietta Johnston, the earliest recorded female artist working in the English colonies, hangs to one side. These four likenesses include Isaac Mazyck, the

grandfather of the woman pictured above the mantel. Other art in the room is more recent, such as a small painting by Alfred Hutty, a leader of the Charleston Renaissance movement, and an oil sketch by Gian Carlo Menotti, founder of the city's annual Spoleto Festival. Taken together, this collection celebrates the generations of people who've made Charleston what it is today.

When the present-day owners purchased the house, the only room lacking in historic material of note was the kitchen. This room was largely shaped by a Works Progress Administration renovation in the 1930s intended to recover what had become a slum property. As a result, the current homeowners felt free to strip it to the studs, leaving only the original heart pine floors and ceiling beams. Industrial lamps hanging above the kitchen island and exposed brick and piping contribute to a modern impression, offset by the historic appearance of the arched brick niche housing the stove. The most imaginative addition is a mural stretching across one full wall that depicts the 1711 "Crisp Map" of Charleston, as well as its surrounding plantation lands. The names and images of land owned by Wilson's ancestors in St. John's Berkeley are incorporated into the mural painted by Karl Beckwith Smith, including Pooshee Plantation, flooded during the construction of Santee Dam in the early twentieth century. When the fate of their cherished home became clear, Wilson's extended family salvaged as much architectural material as possible, including the brick now used to line the house's Queen Street entryway.

The gouge-work mantel in the second-story library also came from Pooshee and its place in the house honors formerly enslaved craftsmen whose work adorned many of the plantation houses now also submerged under Lake Moultrie. Above it hangs a portrait of Wilson's ancestor James Edward Cannon, whose great-grandfather, Nathanial Broughton of Mulberry Plantation, is pictured in the drawing room across the hall in a painting by early eighteenth-century Swiss artist Jeremiah Theus. The large, modern triptych hanging over the library's sofa was painted by the owners' niece, Mariel Capanna, and depicts Charleston, the Santee delta, and Pawleys Island—all important parts of the homeowners' lives.

Beneath the classical denticulated cornice of the drawing room, an eclectic array of furnishings and art sets a comparatively casual scene. Collected by the residents at antiques shows, shops, and auctions, these include a red-leather coffee table, armchairs with gently frayed tapestry, and a soft chair upholstered in faded chintz. Federal-style curtains of tasseled silk refashioned from those that came with the house and a period mantel lend delicacy to the space, balancing a masculine array of art including an early eighteenth-century equestrian portrait that speaks to the owners' long association with horses, hounds, and foxhunting. Like all the chambers in the house, this room demonstrates that revering the past does not preclude savoring the present—but, rather, enriches it.

PAGE 145: Four nearly identical contiguous buildings compose Johnson's Row, upscale tenements constructed in the late eighteenth century by New Yorker William Johnson. Their tinted stucco-over-brick facades are in keeping with Charleston's architectural aesthetics.

PREVIOUS SPREAD: The artwork arranged on the cypress walls of the dwelling's dining room includes an oil portrait of Rick Wilson's ancestress Mary Mazyck, painted circa 1770 in Newport, Rhode Island, and a quartet of pastel portraits by early eighteenth-century American artist Henrietta Johnston.

OPPOSITE: The library's heirlooms include a gouge-work mantel crafted by enslaved artisans circa 1820.

LEFT: An equestrian painting by English artist John Wootton (1682–1764) hanging above the living room mantel reflects the homeowners' passion for foxhunting. The room's eclectic array of antiques includes a twentieth-century leather coffee table, nineteenth-century tapestried armchairs, and a painted Louis XVI-style table. The Federal mantel is original to the house.

ABOVE AND OPPOSITE: Wallpaper from the British firm Lewis & Wood in the Adam's Eden pattern possesses a bold design that stands up to the bedroom's handsomely proportioned paneling and moldings. A seventeenth-century Chippendale double chair echoes the wallpaper's cursive lines.

RIGHT: Charleston artist Karl Beckwith Smith painted a mural based on the Edward "Crisp Map" of South Carolina published in London in 1711, which he embellished with scenes of plantations belonging to Rick Wilson's ancestors.

OPPOSITE: When Sheetrock was removed from the front wall of the kitchen, old brick was revealed, inspiring the residents to create the recessed brick arch around the stove. Pendant lamps from Urban Electric contribute an industrial flavor to the room.

WILLIMAN HOUSE

IN THE LATE eighteenth century, a butcher and tanner named Jacob Williman attained such a degree of prosperity that he commissioned a commodious house on the outskirts of Charleston's South of Broad enclave. Constructed in the late 1780s, the single house is transitional in style, combining both Georgian and Federal designs, such as the graceful fanlight over the piazza door and handsome Georgian paneling within. Considered small by today's standards, the original house doubled in size in the twenty-first century with a rear wing invisible from the street designed by Charleston architect Beau Clowney. The sympathetic addition incorporates elements that complement the original structure's historic materials and details, including floors of antique pine resembling those of the extant rooms. In the new living room, classical Doric pilasters frame doors and sash windows, but the scale of these openings introduces a modern sensibility of architectural transparency. Framing extensive views of the garden's profuse greenery, these banks of windows and glass doors also reference the pavilion-like dwellings in India and the Philippines recalled by homeowner Dr. Gene Howard, who spent early years in both countries.

In colonial and postcolonial Charleston, the influence of the East was nearly omnipresent in the popular blue-and-white Canton china and other export tableware from China, the exotic patterns of chintz and woven

carpets, and the luster of silk. But the routes these goods followed from the ports of Asia to Charleston's docks were usually indirect, tracing patterns of trade established by English merchants. In the case of the Howard residence, the Eastern influence is direct and personal, reflecting the collective experiences of the homeowner, who lived and worked in Asia and Africa; his father, who practiced medicine in India and the Philippines; and his grandparents, who were missionaries to India. As a result, the house is filled with Asian and African artifacts and related books collected by three generations. These inspired the decor of the residents' daughter, Alexandra Howard, an interior designer whose vision for the home inhabited by her father and mother, Elizabeth Howard, reveals dual influences of Charleston and the East.

In the living room housed in the addition, she found color inspiration from the garden designed by her father to resemble the tropical ones of his childhood. Pillows in a spectrum of greens scatter across sofas and chairs, including ones sewn from antique Indian silk and sari fragments. Graphic compositions of Asian bronze and porcelain accent the shelves. In the dining room, Howard coupled the Georgian character of the paneling and antique mahogany furniture with wallpaper by de Gournay from the Early Views of India series. Featuring exotic scenes of temples and elephants and dipped in tea to impart an antique finish, the wallpaper establishes an Anglo-Indian colonial atmosphere. Even while fragments of Chinese screens and a Baluchistan rug from Iran emphasize the Eastern influence, the overall character of the furnishings reflects the interior designer's childhood love for old-style Charleston rooms.

The architectural envelope of the adjoining living room is also Georgian, with its handsome yet simple cornice, wainscoting, and mantelpiece. There, the Asian aspects of the decor feel even more distinct, with antique Indian, Cambodian, Korean, and Chinese furniture and art, including campaign chests, a bas-relief screen, an inlaid lacquered screen, and rice paper drawings accenting the room. A pair of sofas with clean lines and silk-cotton upholstery balances the visual and textural maximalism of these pieces, offering white space and a clean, contemporary aesthetic.

A small library-cum-cabinet of curiosities on the second floor holds the major part of the family collection, including Indian, Egyptian, Tibetan, Burmese, and Vietnamese artwork and related books. This space forms a bridge between two guest rooms in the original part of the house and a new master suite at the rear. Like the dining room, the latter possesses an Anglo-Indian colonial air, with panels of Gracie wallpaper adorned with exotic birds and plants, painted wainscoting, and contents reflecting both Asian and Western taste. Like the family living room directly beneath, the bedroom feels subtly modern due to the architect's use of scale and the interior designer's monochromatic palette. Taken together with all the rooms in the house, this twenty-first-century space manifests the versatility and longevity of Charleston's centuries-old architectural and decorative legacies.

PREVIOUS PAGE: The Rembrandt-red paint that interior designer Alexandra Howard chose for the front door of this late eighteenth-century single house accentuates the details of the contrasting white Federal surround.

OPPOSITE: Georgian paneling lines the walls of the drawing room of this transitional house that combines Georgian and Federal styles. In keeping with the Georgian taste for objects made in or inspired by the Orient, most of the room's art and furnishings are Asian.

RIGHT: Indian sandalwood friezes and gilded Chinese bas-reliefs hang above an antique Korean chest in the drawing room. Anglo-Indian campaign chests, an inlaid lacquered Chinese screen, and a rare Cambodian carved panel are also among inherited or collected pieces decorating the room.

LEFT: The dining room features an unusual, asymmetrical Georgian mantelpiece. The gilded details of a French mirror, bronze Art Nouveau candlesticks, and a late nineteenth-century chandelier highlight the room's neutral palette. Ivory silk covers a set of nineteenth-century Biedermeier-style chairs encircling a reproduction Georgian-style table. Panels of de Gournay's Early Views of India wallpaper were tea-stained to impart an antique appearance.

163

RIGHT: The breakfast room's furnishings, including a weathered-oak French farm table, Gustavian chairs, and a vintage country-French tassel chandelier, possess antique tones and textures that contrast with the kitchen's sleek *Arabescato Corchia* marble countertops.

OPPOSITE: The addition to the 1780s house designed by architect Beau Clowney employs historically inspired paneling and antique heart-pine floorboards that match those of the original dwelling.

RIGHT: With pilasters framing modernly proportioned windows and doors that open to a screened porch, Clowney's design for the family room references traditional architecture while updating it and rendering it less formal. Interior designer Alexandra Howard's palette for the room is drawn from nature, echoing the myriad shades of green in the surrounding garden.

RIGHT: To unite the detailing of the new master bedroom with the house's original rooms, the architect employed Georgian-inspired wainscoting. Alexandra Howard custom-colored panels of Gracie wallpaper in a palette of gold and ivory animated by brightly hued tropical birds. The gold-tinged surfaces of the hammered metal bed frame designed by Oly Studio, lamps fashioned from antique Italian candlesticks, and a nineteenth-century French gilt-wood and cane bench complement the wallpaper's color scheme.

SAMUEL MILLER HOUSE

TRANSPARENCY AND OPENNESS seem to have been on architect and architectural historian Samuel Gaillard Stoney's mind when he designed the 1928 addition to a prerevolutionary house on Orange Street. Passersby can peek through the ironwork of a gate salvaged from an old rice mill and peer through a courtyard to a glass door that frames a view of a luminous loggia and the garden beyond. Light, airy, and engaged with its natural surroundings, this design is quite different from that of the original 1777 structure, which rises straight up from the sidewalk with no trace of a portico or piazza to bridge the interior and exterior spaces. Like many of Charleston's eighteenth-century houses, this one was built close to its immediate neighbors, precluding the possibility of a piazza or side garden. It was not until one of the adjacent houses was moved that an opportunity arose to expand the footprint of the house and embrace the surroundings.

The original house was built by Samuel Miller, a carpenter and son of a carpenter, who demonstrated his talents within. The facade of the house he built was solid and sensible, constructed of brick with no ornament save a simple cornice beneath the eaves of a tile roof. Plentiful, tall, nine-over-nine-pane windows prevent the facade from appearing overly severe and bring natural illumination and ventilation into the rooms within. Today, stucco with a deep patina of sepia and rose, accented by aqua-colored shutters, lend the

house a romantic, tropical air. The chalky pink brick wall and blue-green gate of the adjacent courtyard and auto court echo the palette, uniting the disparate parts of the property.

In keeping with the single-house model associated with Charleston, the house is one room wide and two rooms deep, with the narrow end facing the street. With bedrooms above, the ground floor rooms were intended for daily living and entertaining. The drawing room on the first floor was also likely a place for Miller to conduct business and showcased his skills as a carpenter, both in the handsome cypress paneling and ornamentation of the mantel. Outlined with classical dentils, the unusual mantel includes panels with a raised pattern of vines and flowers that also appears in silhouette as a hand-carved grille on the nearby door.

Interior designer Athalie Derse was drawn to the house by the rich and varied character of the spaces, from the intimacy of the original drawing room and dining room to the indoor-outdoor quality of the loggia designed by Stoney. Enclosed with windows and Dutch doors, the loggia is a light-filled connector that parallels a charming courtyard to join the front of the house with another addition added in 1964. A place to pass through multiple times a day, it is one of Derse's favorite rooms in the house.

Taking a cue from Stoney's vision of the space as a gardenesque corridor, she decorated it with plaster torchieres with a palm frond motif and Mediterranean-style iron-frame chairs that have occupied the porches of her previous homes.

In the drawing room, now a study, the interior designer was inspired by the amber-toned paneling to create a comfortable, cozy room. While Charlestonians of decades past might have felt compelled to decorate the space in traditional style, with antiques, heavy drapery, and an Oriental rug, Derse combined a vintage knole sofa, mid-century modern pendant lamp, Albert Hadley table, and grass mat to create a personal, collected look. The only antiques in the room are an eighteenth-century French secretary and a splat-back chair.

Although the adjoining sitting room, originally the dining room, is also paneled, it had been brightened with paint by the time Derse and her husband acquired the house. The room also features French doors that connect it with the courtyard lying just a few steps below its floor. Inspired by the room's relationship with the natural world, Derse decorated it in tones of blue and green that echo the outdoor palette of sky and vegetation. A poem of past and present, light and shadow, embrace and expansiveness, the house is singular in style but universal in appeal.

PREVIOUS PAGE: Built in 1777 as the home to carpenter Samuel Miller, the original single house was enlarged when a neighboring edifice was moved, creating space for a courtyard entrance and recessed addition designed by well-known Charleston architectural historian Samuel Stoney in 1928.

OPPOSITE: The addition includes an enclosed loggia that overlooks an interior courtyard.

RIGHT: Samuel Miller demonstrated his carpenter's skill in the drawing room with cypress paneling and an unusual flower-and-vine motif carved on the mantel and neighboring door. Interior designer Athalie Derse furnished the room as a cozy study with eclectic furnishings including an eighteenth-century French secretary, mid-century modern pendant lamp, and lacquered coffee table designed by Albert Hadley.

RIGHT: With French doors opening to the courtyard, the small dining room on the first floor of the original house possesses an airy atmosphere. A pair of French sofas, circa 1800, facing a papier-mâché travel table creates an elegant and inviting seating area.

OPPOSITE: The rear facade of the 1777 house and the 1928 loggia form two sides of a secluded courtyard.

RIGHT: A lantern from the Pabst brewing family's Wisconsin summer estate, likely used in a loggia, hangs in the center of the main bedroom, which also includes a fireside seating area with tufted chairs from Quigley Furniture Company, a Maison Jansen folding bench, and a painting by Charleston artist Anne Parker.

OPPOSITE: Derse chose a calm, tonal palette with a paint color that shifts from celadon green to aqueous blue through-out the day. The black of antique coromandel screens and the painted bonnet of a nineteenth-century American bed balance the ethereal scheme.

POINSETT TAVERN

FROM TAVERN TO apothecary to dilapidated tenement to elegantly restored home, the Poinsett Tavern's story recounts the rise, fall, and resurrection of Charleston's South of Broad district in colorful detail. Built in the early 1700s by the Poinsett family, the tavern served grog to pirates smoking pipes etched with skulls and crossbones and hosted gatherings raising funds for needy Huguenot immigrants. Partially destroyed by fire in 1778, it was rebuilt to continue service as a tavern and subsequently an apothecary shop for Dr. Elisha Poinsett, for whose son, noted naturalist Joel Roberts Poinsett, the poinsettia is named. Following the Civil War, the once affluent neighborhood languished, with its buildings declining into slum tenements with as many as twenty families living in houses such as one nearby.

By 1940, the former tavern acquired new owners riding the tide of Charleston's preservationist movement, which had spurred interest in protecting and restoring the city's period architecture. During this time, skilled African-American artisans, many of whom learned their trade from fathers and enslaved grandfathers, were valued for their knowledge and talents. Thomas Mayhem Pinckney, son of cabinetmaker Nathaniel Pinckney, was one such artisan highly skilled in hand-carved woodwork. Frequently employed by Susan Pringle Frost, mother of Charleston's preservation movement, Pinckney

found time to restore and re-create Georgian-style paneling on the first and second floors of the old tavern. Today, the paneling survives, complemented by a modern bay of windows in the dining room and a glass-and-steel balcony on the second floor designed by Charleston architect Eddie Fava.

The present-day owners were attracted to the building's historic material and high ceilings that mitigate the limited light entering from the front and rear elevations. This height allowed the architect to elevate door openings, permitting light to travel throughout and establishing a subtly modern sensibility. The architect also added the dining room's glass bay that measures only thirty-two inches deep but succeeds in transforming the space into an airy room addressing the garden. In the chamber above, Pinckney's Georgian-style paneling lines a space with large windows and French doors that open to the glass-and-steel balcony overlooking the garden and the guesthouse. The latter, constructed of antique brick found on the property on the site of the original kitchen house, informed the living room's palette of warm terra-cotta tones.

Large acrylic tables and sleek chairs find a place in this setting, but many of the furnishings in the room are antiques. An eighth-generation descendant of an eastern North Carolina family, one of the present-day homeowners sees her approach to design as a continuation of her ancestors' story. Throughout the property, family heirlooms stand side by side with modern pieces in an environment that at times feels contemporary in spirit. The mid-eighteenth-century repoussé pitcher that reflects light from the dining room's glass bay belonged to this resident's great-grandmother. The living room's mirror with a gessoed, foliated frame, a cherished hand-me-down from a great-great-aunt, injects a flourish of whimsy amid the room's stately paneling. The acrylic coffee tables were custom designed by the homeowner with the help of a contemporary craftsman in New York. Textiles chosen with the guidance of interior designers Katherine Matthews and Athalie Derse complement and update their antique surroundings throughout the house. In the guesthouse, a portrait of one of the residents' great-great-grandfathers hangs in a room accented by a sleek, new spiral stair.

The modern aesthetic at play in the house enjoys full expression in the garden, even as antique objects still find their place. The design accentuates the linear quality of the attenuated, narrow garden with a slender concrete monolith standing at the end of an allée that travels from the street through a bricked passage. Softened by a cascade of water, it silhouettes a classical urn. A second axis parallel to the dining room terminates in another contemporary fountain featuring an urn flanked by English mileposts in the form of herms. Visually cooling the space, bluestone replaces the original brick paving. Overlooked by the main house's handmade bricks, new bay, and steel-and-glass balcony on one side, and the guesthouse's old brick and plate-glass windows on the other, this garden room brings the past and present into play. Like the structures that border the space, it combines evidence of many generations with ease, expressing the spirit of the city in which it stands—a place where layers of centuries gracefully coexist.

PREVIOUS PAGE AND OPPOSITE: Originally a tavern, this house possesses a covered carriageway leading from the street into an inner courtyard paved with bluestone. Within the courtyard stands a guesthouse constructed of antique brick found on the property and modernized with plate-glass windows and a contemporary spiral staircase.

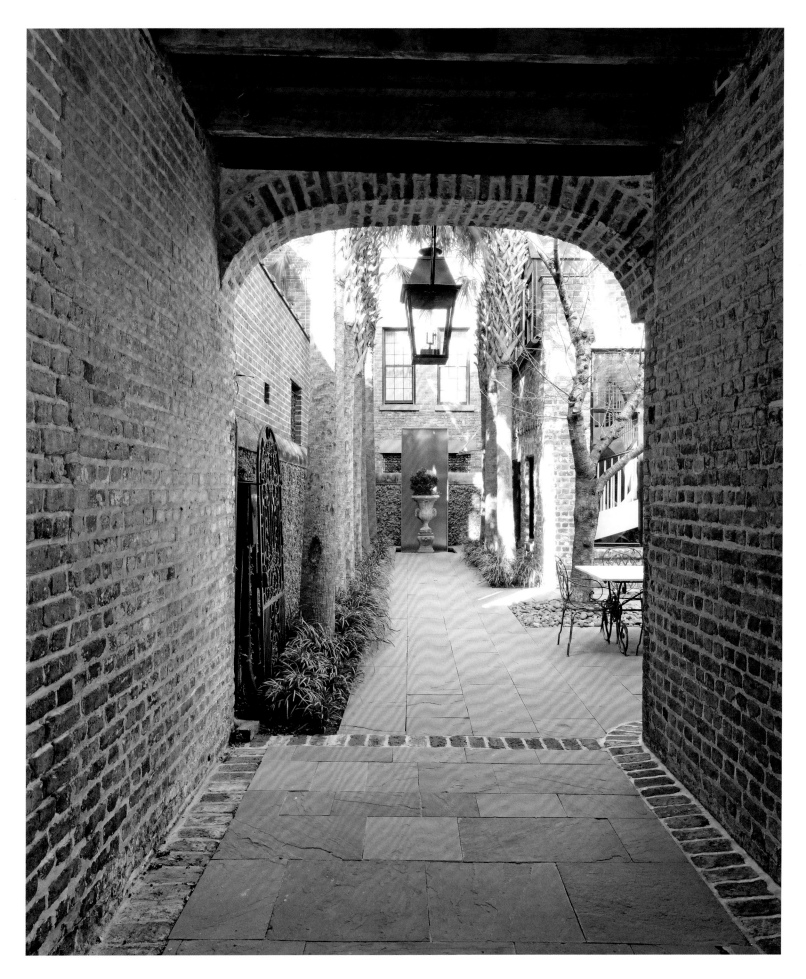

OPPOSITE: Architect Eddie Fava designed the window bay and balcony that enhances the relationship between the interior of the main house and the courtyard.

LEFT: With Fava's expertise, the homeowners fulfilled their vision of a cool, calming garden. A fountain that marries a monolithic slab of concrete with a sculptural antique urn reflects the property's antique-meets-modern sensibility.

RIGHT: A recess beside the dining room's fireplace provides a luminous niche where the grain of an early nineteenth-century chest and the surface of a repoussé pitcher can catch the light.

OPPOSITE: Panels of antique French wallpaper depicting a fishing scene in Brittany forge a colorful connection with Charleston's coastal setting.

RIGHT: Georgian-style paneling crafted in the early twentieth century by African-American carpenter Thomas Mayhem Pinckney assumes an almost modern air in the white-painted living room. Antique furniture with warm wood grain offers counterpoint to modern pieces including contemporary sconces, acrylic coffee tables, and a painting by Italian artist Riccardo Baruzzi.

RIGHT: Framed by one of a pair of niches flanking the fireplace, the silhouettes of a French-style chair and contemporary oval sconce complement the organic lines of Baruzzi's painting.

OPPOSITE: In the stair hall, a reproduction French console table designed by Carleton Varney shares space with a sculptural cast-stone stool.

RIGHT: When the home-owners remodeled the guesthouse with Fava's aid, modern paneling was removed to expose the old brick walls and Sheetrock was taken out to raise the ceiling and reveal the original joists. Polished Belgian bluestone flooring, a plate-glass window, and sleek contemporary spiral stair contrast with highly textured antique surfaces.

GEORGE EVELEIGH HOUSE

FIRMITATIS. UTILITATIS. VENUSTATIS. These words are inscribed above a door in the twenty-first-century addition to a 1743 dwelling standing on a bend of historic Church Street. These three principles of architecture—strength, functionality, and beauty—were defined over two millennia ago by Roman architect Vitruvius, whose writings have influenced the field ever since. From the British neoclassical periods of Georgian and Adamesque architecture to the buildings these inspired in America, they have found expression over a period of more than three centuries and continue to influence the neo-traditional movement of today. In this house, home to multiple generations of Charlestonians, from its first owner George Eveleigh, a deerskin trader, to the present-day homeowners who have done much to preserve and enhance it, these principles stand strong.

Every generation has a different viewpoint concerning the function and design of a house and its rooms, as the slight asymmetry of the facade of the Eveleigh House attests. Originally, the pillared brick entry gate led directly to a central door opening into one of the two rooms spanning the front of the house. Deeming a foyer a fashionable necessity, a nineteenth-century resident had the door moved to one side so that it opened into an entrance hall, as it does today. In the early twentieth century, when a family of Charlestonians

PAGE 195: As an indication of wealth and fashion, George Eveleigh had the facade of his house constructed with brick imported from England, allowing the less visible side and rear walls to be built from Charleston-made brick.

LEFT: In the morning room, interior designer Amelia Handegan united disparate furnishings including an eighteenth-century Venetian sofa and a pair of mid-century modern slipper chairs by employing velvet upholstery in related tones.

who hosted sizable gatherings for holiday meals occupied the house, two rooms across the back of the house were joined to create a single large dining room. Today, these chambers are once again distinct, affording the current residents an intimate dining room adjoining a secondary space for serving and gathering.

Documents suggest that the foyer's walls were originally covered in silk—a sign of luxury in an era when importing textiles from Asia was an expensive enterprise. Today, its walls are once again covered with silk in a golden hue that complements the duskier shades of the adjacent morning room. Interior designer Amelia Handegan selected this wall covering, along with sumptuous curtains and upholstery throughout the house, where shades of sepia and topaz warm rooms with Georgian-raised paneling tinted ivory, gold, and celadon.

Fine art collected by one of the homeowners, an art dealer, enhances the classical grace and tonalities of these surroundings. In the morning room, a circa-1960s portrait by French painter André Minaux surmounts the mantelpiece, introducing twentieth-century energy to the setting. An early nineteenth-century ancestral portrait hangs in the dining room, diagonally across from a portrait by Thomas Sully. A modern-day likeness by classically trained American painter Charles Weed adds luster to the foyer, and above the stair's wainscoting, drawings dating from the eighteenth century to the present mingle.

When the current residents replaced an old kitchen and bathroom extension across the rear of the house, they commissioned an architectural work of art by Christopher Liberatos, a classically trained architect who brings the rigor of Vitruvius, Palladio, and their Georgian and Federal offspring to his work. To accommodate a modern kitchen and breakfast room below and master bath above, he conceived of a space resembling an elegantly enclosed porch. Incorporating the original brick rear wall of the house into the design, he added a screen of French doors with sidelights and transoms that overlook the garden. On the lower floor, fluted pilasters with a rusticated wood finish and dentil moldings complement the classical style of the house while contrasting with the sleek stone and metal of the modern kitchen.

Viewed from the exterior, the addition bears even greater resemblance to a porch with engaged Doric columns and a balustrade that quote typical features of the Charleston piazza. Its bright white paint offers dazzling contrast to the patina of the surrounding masonry surfaces of brick walls and the stucco facade of the circa-1850 kitchen house, now a guesthouse. Together, these architectural elements surround a garden, which, though small in size, offers an invitation to stroll along shady paths or linger on a terrace just outside the kitchen doors. Designed in the early twentieth century by Loutrel Briggs, the favored landscape architect of Charleston's colonial revival era, and still adhering to his plan, this garden epitomizes Vitruvius's timeless principles of strength, functionality, and beauty, echoing the character of the house it graces.

RIGHT: As an art dealer and collector with a preference for figurative art, one of the homeowners selected portraits dating from the eighteenth century to the present, including works by contemporary Italian artist Daniela Astone, above, and classically trained artist Charles Weed, below, in the entrance hall.

OPPOSITE: In a small room adjoining the dining room, the pattern of Gracie wallpaper complements the lithe subject of a nineteenth-century portrait by Thomas Sully.

RIGHT: When the residents reconstructed a wall in order to restore the dining room to its original configuration, they hired historic restoration expert Richard Marks to copy the 1758 paneling. In the process, they discovered a panel signed by eighteenth-century carpenter Joseph Veree. English Regency chairs with ebonized wood-and-gilt frames and a French Empire chandelier contribute both depth and highlights to their dusky gold-toned surroundings.

FIRMITATIS · UTILITATIS · VENUSTATIS

ABOVE: Architect Christopher Liberatos designed an addition to the rear of the house to accommodate a modern kitchen and breakfast room. The three principles of architecture defined by Roman classical architect Vitruvius in *De Architectura* are inscribed in Latin above French doors opening to the garden.

OPPOSITE: Liberatos incorporated the original rear wall of the house into the design to create the impression of an enclosed porch.

RIGHT: Charleston's preeminent mid-twentieth-century landscape architect Loutrel Briggs designed the walled garden, which though small, contains multiple elements including parterres, shady paths, a burbling fountain, and a paved seating area.

OPPOSITE: The engaged columns and second-floor railing of Liberatos's design resemble elements of latterly enclosed nineteenth-century porches.

ANNE BOONE HOUSE

Situated on Charleston's East Battery, the Anne Boone House is both a resilient survivor and an example of the architectural reinvention that lies at the heart of the city's enduring style. The house was reconstructed circa 1740–1749 within the brick shell of an extant dwelling that survived the 1740 fire that destroyed most of the surrounding waterfront buildings. At the time of the fire, the damage to the house was reckoned at more than six hundred pounds sterling, indicating a near-total loss of its value. However, the burned-out structure was reclaimed to become what is considered the earliest example of the Charleston single house. With its gable end facing the street and its entrance centered on the lateral facade, the exterior typifies the vernacular form. Expressing other aspects of the single house, the central door opens to a stair hall flanked by rooms on either side, an arrangement that allows for windows on three sides to maximize exposure to cooling breezes.

The restored house was the home of Anne Boone, daughter of a Puritan refugee who was among the immigrants welcomed by Charleston's Lords Proprietors. Boone's husband, also a Puritan, played a prominent role in the colony's varied political struggles. Little is known about Boone herself except that she bequeathed the property to her husband's nephews who later transferred it to the family of prosperous cotton planter William Roper, who resided

there until 1753. It was not until 1840 that further renovations contributed another iconic aspect of the Charleston single house—a long porch, or piazza, perpendicular to the street and entered from the sidewalk through a classically embellished door. Over time, the house also acquired an iron balcony original to another house and, after bearing the brunt of 1989's Hurricane Hugo, required major restoration resulting in a nineteenth-century-style closed pediment profile.

The current owner, interior decorator Ceara Donnelley, was intrigued by the house's extensive original material and saw in it the perfect setting for her signature style of combining the old with the new. With architect Glenn Keyes and restoration contractor Richard Marks, she redesigned the original kitchen house that was attached by a twentieth-century connector and added a breakfast room that replaced a portion of the piazza removed by a previous resident. While complementing the original house, these parts also reveal a contemporary aesthetic with walls and banks of windows rendering them lighter and more transparent than the adjoining rooms. This is particularly evident in the breakfast room, where walls and folding doors of glass create a luminous space that dissolves into the surrounding gardens.

Donnelley's aesthetic comes into full focus in the ground-floor drawing room where Georgian paneling and an 1820 Regency mantel provide a traditional backdrop for mid-century Italian pieces, including Aldo Tura side tables and a ram's head coffee table. A groovy 1970s Luna Lamp and carved Lucite table by Harlem-based artist Joyce Frances offer counterpoint to the room's nineteenth-century Louis XIV *bureau plat* desk and japanned armoire. All favorite heirlooms or acquisitions of the resident, these

pieces come together in a composition that expresses outside-of-the-box thinking to create a mood of lighthearted harmony.

The dining room on the other side of the hall is a slightly more serious room with strié walls in a shade reminiscent of the faded green rooms of the Georgian plantation house Drayton Hall. A large mirror in an eighteenth-century Irish-style frame hanging above the Regency mantel contributes to the historic character of the room, but the fanciful form of Elkins Loop chairs, a peacock-shaped chandelier reproduced after a Tony Duquette original, and the rug's snake and pomegranate motif are far from staid.

In a similarly unconventional style, the withdrawing room on the second floor displays glossy plum-colored paint on its eighteenth-century cypress paneling and colorful ikat-style curtains around its windows. Once a room for formal entertaining, this now functions as a family gathering space and also serves as a library, with walls of built-in bookcases designed, like all the recent architectural changes, to be reversed without damage to the original material of the house. Playful without being irreverent, contemporary without losing sight of the rich history of the house, Donnelley's twenty-first-century reimagining offers a perfect modern-day chapter to this unique structure's rich history.

PREVIOUS PAGE: Inspired by Moroccan *moucharabiya*, the open-work cabinetry on the second-floor offers a trellislike appearance that complements the organic forms of majolica plates. An artful porcelain vase possesses eyes that gaze toward the room's four entrances.

OPPOSITE: Working with architect Glenn Keyes, Ceara Donnelley created an enclosed first-floor dining room and second-story sitting room at the rear of the piazza. Engaged Doric columns unite the addition with the 1840s design of the porch.

RIGHT: A carved Lucite table by Joyce Francis and three-dimensional artwork above the mantel inject modern energy into the Georgian-paneled drawing room.

OPPOSITE: Although separated by centuries of style, the fluid lines of 1960s swivel chairs and a Louis XIV *bureau plat* complement each other. The curvy silhouettes of a gilt-frame sofa and contemporary tufted one offer softening contrast to the paneling's straight lines.

ABOVE: The muted green strié wall treatment of the room is intended to recall the patina of paneling in Drayton Hall's entertaining rooms.

OPPOSITE: Majolica geese found in a local antiques shop, Elkins Loop chairs, and a fanciful chandelier reproduced after a Tony Duquette original bring a lighthearted spirit to the gravitas of the dining room's formal architecture.

LEFT: A Saarinen tulip table and white-painted Thonet chairs cushioned in a botanical motif create a fresh vignette that visually connects the family dining room with the surrounding piazza and garden. Bifold doors open the room to the elements, allowing the residents to enjoy an alfresco dining experience.

RIGHT: Glossy aubergine paint updates the Georgian cypress paneling of the library, which also serves as the family gathering space. Schumacher ikat-style curtains, a mid-century modern parchment cabinet, and a painting by Charleston modernist William Halsey introduce pattern into the room while a capacious mohair sectional quiets the space.

OPPOSITE: Ceara Donnelley designed a tester bed that provides a safe-from-children-and-dogs place to employ opulent silk damask. The luxurious fabric inspired the palette for a master bedroom decorated in serene shades of yellow, amber, and cream.

LEFT: In one corner of the room, a chaise longue with soft velvet upholstery issues an invitation to leisurely reclining.

A 1930s BUNGALOW

THE YOUNGEST HOUSE on the block, this circa-1930 bungalow shares few of the characteristics of nearby Charleston single houses. Welcoming steps leading toward an unobscured entrance porch distinguish it from nearby dwellings with street-front doors opening to long, secluded piazzas. While typical single houses are replete with classical detail, from Doric, Ionic, and Corinthian columns to decorative porticoes and pediments, only a bare hint of classicism is evinced here by the pillars supporting the facade's tall, undecorated frieze. Despite these differences, the floor plan within functions much like that of a Charleston single house and its decor reflects the relaxed elegance that characterizes the city's approach to interior design.

Shielding the windows of the adjacent living room by allowing only filtered light and shade-cooled air within, the entrance porch functions similarly to the Charleston piazza. Also in common with the single house plan, the front door opens into a center hall that is surprisingly wide for this modestly scaled home. In a traditional arrangement, tall entrances on either side of the hall lead to living and dining rooms and a handsome stair climbs to the second floor. The hall is so spacious that it serves as an additional entertaining space during large gatherings and affords enough room for a correspondence desk beneath the large window opposite the stair.

PREVIOUS PAGE: An air of casual elegance pervades the living room where a portrait by nineteenth-century painter Thomas Sully shares space with silk curtains that cascade to meet sisal rugs and contrast with informally slip-covered chairs.

RIGHT: Built in the early twentieth century, the house possesses restrained classical elements including simple Doric pillars and pilasters.

OPPOSITE: Scenting the air, fragrant jasmine vines frame the entrance to the lower porch.

The architectural details of the interior are restrained, with simple trim around walls, ceilings, and doorways. This provided the home-owner, an interior designer, the perfect canvas to practice her personal preference for mixing the antique with the modern and the formal with the informal. She used a shade of paint for the living room that is a touch more chartreuse in hue and modern in feel than the classic Georgian green. Sisal rugs cover the room's floor and much of the furniture is slip-covered in white linen. The relaxed atmosphere calls to mind early Charlestonians' summertime practice of replacing fine carpets with grass rugs and draping furniture with sheets to protect them from light and insects. In this modern-day residence, these materials give the room a year-round livable air and provide a perfect backdrop for the refined lines and gleaming surfaces of antique furniture, Southern art, and silver bibelots.

The antiques throughout the house, primarily English, hint at Charleston's formal decorative traditions, in which fine furniture imported from Europe and England was highly prized. The most important antique in the living room, however, claims American provenance—an early nineteenth-century portrait by Thomas Sully, who hailed from Charleston and painted many of its grandees. The room also includes an expressive drawing of an African-American basket weaver by Albert Hutty, one of the twentieth-century artists drawn to the city by its poignant, post-Civil War atmosphere. More paintings and drawings of African-American subjects can be found throughout the house in testimony to the long, at times tragic, intermingling of black and white lives in the South.

In the entrance hall, a carved head of an African woman stands on a skirted console alongside a Chinese ceremonial necklace and a carved stone figure of the Egyptian cat goddess Bastet. Indonesian replicas of Regency chairs, a Turkish rug, and a Buddha figure poised on a nineteenth-century southern European desk reveal a sensibility shaped by travel and curiosity. This global attitude was an important aspect of affluent, antebellum Charleston style, when travel, study of European architecture, collecting art and artifacts from around the world, and displaying them throughout the home signaled a cosmopolitan way of life. Globes were, in fact, a popular fixture in gentlemen's libraries.

Excepting the leopard-print rug and contemporary starburst pendant chosen in lieu of a crystal chandelier, the dining room is the most recognizably Charleston in appearance. Pieces of fine blue-and-white Canton china and a silver gallery tray laden with crystal and silver form a classic tableau atop a richly grained mahogany sideboard from England. Inherited objects of silver and crystal, a Canton vase, and a pair of Chinese figures stand atop a chest attributed to Duncan Phyfe. Across the room, a silver pitcher that belonged to the interior designer's mother, from which she remembers drinking iced tea every day as a child, sits on an Italian chest beneath a drawing by modern master Otto Neumann. A native Southerner, the resident jokes that she does not worship her ancestors, but simply honors them by displaying the things she has inherited in plain sight in a way that keeps them relevant today.

OPPOSITE: A leopard-print rug balances the formality of the dining room's English and Continental European furniture that includes this graceful English eighteenth-century table and antique English stool. Canton china and shimmering silver and crystal offer bright contrast to the dark palette of the room's antique wood and nineteenth-century romantic paintings.

OPPOSITE: The residents removed a wall and door beside the fireplace to unite the living room and sunroom into a larger, more flexible area that functions well for both intimate occasions and larger gatherings. Most of the furniture is upholstered in plain linen, which allows the rich grain of wooden chests and portraits to speak eloquently.

ABOVE: The embellishment of the mantel features a sensitive portrait of an African-American woman drawn by Alfred Hutty, a Woodstock, New York–based artist considered the founder of the early twentieth-century Charleston Renaissance.

LEFT: In the hall, which serves as an ancillary entertaining area during parties, the residents re-created an original gold fillet at the top of the walls to enhance its elegance. Furnishings in the large hall include contemporary lighting and an eighteenth-century French writing table.

RIGHT: Heirlooms in the
dining room include
a chest attributed to
Duncan Phyfe, an identi-
cal twin to one exhibited
in the Metropolitan
Museum of Art, and
a pair of eighteenth-
century Chinese figures.

OPPOSITE: Golden hues
unite items as disparate
as a gilt-framed drawing
by German Expressionist
Otto Neumann, a
contemporary starburst
chandelier, an Old Paris
porcelain lamp, and a
decorative assemblage of
cut glass, coral, and brass.

RIGHT: Affording a view of rooftops and a canopy of oak trees, the second-floor porch provides a comfortable vantage point from which to appreciate Charleston's charms. Centered above the rattan sofa, sconce-like lanterns and a mirror framed by squares of antique pressed tin lend the semi-enclosed area a roomlike impression.

ADDITIONAL CAPTIONS

PAGE 2: Glimpsed through an iron gate's design of intersecting ovals and arches, a garden's palette of green boxwood and white gravel recalls French and English neo-classical designs and offers respite from Charleston's heat.

PAGE 4: The velvet upholstery of a nineteenth-century recamier sofa issues an invitation to relax within the formal setting of the Edmondston-Alston House's drawing room. Asymmetrical drapery accentuates the beauty of carved window surrounds, and folding interior blinds shield the interior from bright light.

PAGES 6-7: Most of the houses along Charleston's East Battery possess side porches, known locally as piazzas, designed to capture sea breezes and provide shade for the interior. The pink-stuccoed Edmondston-Alston House is also equipped with triple-sash windows that offer access to a covered balcony on the second-floor drawing room.

PAGE 16: During the Federal period, to which the Nathaniel Russell House has been faithfully restored, strong wall color, often with decorative trim, was the fashion as shown in this bedroom. Inspired by the Chinese Canton china readily available in Charleston, blue and white was a favorite color combination, especially in textiles with Asian-influenced patterns.

PAGE 17, UPPER LEFT: A gilt-framed mirror and silver card cases gleam like jewelry against chartreuse paint reminiscent of Georgian green. **UPPER RIGHT:** Historical research revealed that the Nathaniel Russell House's dining room was papered in a vibrant shade of blue with contrasting trim. **LOWER LEFT:** The wood carving and wainscoting of Drayton Hall's dramatic staircase was once painted a brilliant vermilion hue. **LOWER RIGHT:** A saffron-colored pillow with darker gold passementerie echoes the patina of a nineteenth-century French carved gilt-wood sofa.

PAGE 24: The hand-carved wood moldings of the Miles Brewton House, completed in 1769, represent a pinnacle of Charleston craftsmanship. Several carvers, most trained in England, executed the designs which, though composed of elements published in eighteenth-century style guides, were creatively interpreted and combined.

PAGE 25, UPPER LEFT: The door dividing the vestibule of the Nathaniel Russell House from the inner sanctum of family life and entertaining features an exquisitely crafted screen of carved wood and bentwood and antique glass. **UPPER RIGHT:** A hand-carved cornice of triglyphs and flowers ornaments the paneled walls of Drayton Hall's great hall. The plaster medallion, the third rendition to grace a ceiling that suffered damage over time, reprises the cornice's pattern of flowers. **LOWER LEFT:** In houses of the Georgian era, mantels like this one at Drayton Hall afforded opportunities to further embellish rooms with expertly designed and crafted wood carving. **LOWER RIGHT:** Walls made of bricks handmade by enslaved Africans form an essential and handsome aspect of Charleston's building craft tradition.

PAGE 30: Overgrown with a tangle of fragrant jasmine, this Church Street gate beckons to passersby even as it offers privacy to those in the garden beyond.

PAGE 31, UPPER LEFT: The widely spaced bars of the gate of the Calhoun Mansion, built circa 1876, invite those who stroll by to admire its Italianate facade and manicured garden. **UPPER RIGHT:** This scene combines the harmonious textures of moss-covered brick, variegated masonry, and painted iron that characterize Charleston's historic lanes. **LOWER LEFT:** Charleston's craftsmen transformed bands of iron into sinuous forms like the rosette, spirals, and S-curves of this gate. **LOWER RIGHT:** A white picket gate complements the wooden railings and columns of a neoclassical porch.

PAGE 36: With its grass matting, bamboo furniture, and lush surroundings, this newly constructed screened porch combines the architectural clarity of the Federal-era dwelling it appends with the breeziness of a South Asian veranda.

PAGE 37, UPPER LEFT: While a fanciful garden bench with a latticework back unites this porch with its garden surroundings, the blue-and-white platter and pillow bring a favorite indoor Charleston color combination outdoors. **UPPER RIGHT:** At the Aiken-Rhett House, stucco resembling masonry blocks and a monumental Greek Revival door surround give the piazza a majestic air. **LOWER LEFT:** In Charleston, the street entrances to houses often open to their piazzas. **LOWER RIGHT:** Porch-side doors and windows are equipped with louvered shutters designed to be adjusted according to the weather and the angle of the sun.

PAGE 42: With front doors opening to porches instead of interior halls or rooms, the Charleston single house offers an unusual entrance sequence that blurs the boundaries between indoor and outdoor spaces.

PAGE 43: Whether Georgian, Federal, or Greek Revival, Charleston's front doors frequently feature broken pediments decorated with dentils and supported by pilasters. Fanlights with intricate muntins are often incorporated, bringing light into the entrance hall and contributing beauty to the streetscape.

PAGE 48: With slender pilasters that appear to balance on a base of gilded balls and are crowned with gilded leaf-shaped capitals, the window surrounds in the Nathaniel Russell House's withdrawing room illustrate the exquisite delicacy and imagination of Federal-era architects and designers.

PAGE 49, UPPER LEFT: In addition to being functional, decorative gilt curtain knobs like these in the Nathaniel Russell House were de rigueur in the elegant eighteenth- and nineteenth-century room. UPPER RIGHT: In the English Regency–style Edmondston-Alston House, rope- and pearl-bead molding provides decorative interest to windows and doors. LOWER LEFT: Lavish drapery and passementerie add vivid contrast to the blue walls of the Nathaniel Russell House's dining room. LOWER RIGHT: In the Miles Brewton House's north parlor, gilded eagles enhance the drama of red-and-gold cornice boards.

PAGE 54: With folding shutters that recess into surrounding paneling, architectural designer Andrew Gould replicated a typical Georgian feature in his dining room.

PAGE 55, UPPER LEFT: At the Aiken-Rhett House, remnants of nineteenth-century French wallpaper still adorn the walls of the double parlor. UPPER RIGHT: In keeping with Charleston's nineteenth-century penchant for scenic wallpaper, interior designer Alexandra Howard chose de Gourney's Early Views of India pattern to adorn a dining room. LOWER LEFT: Faithfully reproduced orange-and-white wallpaper trim outlines the verditer blue walls of the Miles Brewton House's library. LOWER RIGHT: Massive gilded pier mirrors magnify the drama of the Aiken-Rhett House's drawing room, where faded remnants of nineteenth-century gold- and silver-trimmed flocked wallpaper survive.

PAGE 58: The free-flying stair that ascends through three stories of the Nathaniel Russell House with no visible means of support is considered one of the finest examples of Federal staircases in America.

PAGE 59, UPPER LEFT: Meticulous craftsmanship was required to create the curves and spirals of the Nathaniel Russell House's mahogany stair rail. UPPER RIGHT: Although monumentally scaled, the radiating forms of the plaster medallion that crowns the stair of the Joseph Manigault House are delicately executed. LOWER LEFT: Brick steps lead to the site where Middleton Place plantation's main house, built 1705, once stood. LOWER RIGHT: Masterfully carved stone adds shapely curves to the front steps of a house in downtown Charleston.

PAGE 66: Simple overmantel detailing in the Georgian style complements the restrained mantlepiece in the paneled drawing room of the Williman House, constructed in the late 1780s.

PAGE 67, UPPER LEFT: A gouge-work mantel executed by an African-American craftsman was salvaged from the homeowner's ancestral plantation. UPPER RIGHT: The

residents removed an Adamesque mantel that did not complement this room's Georgian paneling, replacing it with period-style bolection moldings. LOWER LEFT: The original carved wood mantel of the Miles Brewton House's north parlor was moved to an upper room when marble mantelpieces came into vogue. LOWER RIGHT: Delft tiles were a popular mode of ornamentation for mantels in the Georgian era as shown here in the Poinsett Tavern's dining room.

PAGE 74: A dramatic gilt-wood mirror in the Hewyard-Washington House's drawing room reflects the baroque era's penchant for decorative objects inspired by Asian forms and occasionally, asymmetrical, organic lines.

PAGE 75, UPPER LEFT: An early nineteenth-century mahogany pianoforte with rosewood and satinwood veneer recalls the importance of musical entertainment in rooms like the east drawing room of the Edmondston-Alston House. UPPER RIGHT: When William and Harriet Aiken embarked on a yearlong Grand Tour in the mid-nineteenth century, they collected European art, some antique and some copies, to display in a gallery they added to their house. LOWER RIGHT: The residents of the Poinsett Tavern decorated it with heirlooms throughout the house, including this circa 1840 repoussé pitcher and candlesticks acquired at the London silver vaults. LOWER RIGHT: In the early nineteenth century, it was fashionable to purchase furniture constructed in England, such as this London-made chair in the collection of the Nathaniel Russell House.

PAGE 80: A long eighteenth-century English table does double duty in a dining room as a server and a place to display a collection of china, crystal, and silver pieces, such as these heirloom Canton china plates, English crystal, and silver goblet.

PAGE 81, UPPER LEFT: Cut glass, such as this heirloom pitcher with goblets, is prized by Southerners for its sparkling facets as well as its utility. UPPER RIGHT: A Chinese import vase with blue-and-white motifs ornaments the walls of an eighteenth-century dining room. LOWER LEFT: An unusual nineteenth-century repoussé pitcher that pivots on its stand is an eye-catching dining-room accessory. LOWER RIGHT: Early nineteenth-century Worcester porcelain from the English company Flight Barr and Barr brings pattern and color to the Aiken-Rhett House dining room.

PAGES 84–85: Built in 1747 for deer hide trader George Eveleigh, this house sits on a brick-paved street surrounded by old oaks and stucco-over-brick garden walls.

ACKNOWLEDGMENTS

Charleston's allure is a complex amalgam of time, place, material, labor, and imagination. Over a period of three and a half centuries, people have been envisioning Charleston, building Charleston, and protecting her. Thanks go to all the many people whose names we know, as well as even greater gratitude to the enslaved persons whose names we don't. This book would not exist without that rich, tangible history and the ongoing contribution of history-conscious architects and interior designers working today. I am especially grateful to all the homeowners who graciously shared their homes and gave of their time as we worked together to create this book. Heartfelt thanks are also extended to the staff of the historic museum properties featured, particularly Valerie Perry of the Historic Charleston Foundation, Patricia Lowe Smith of Drayton Hall, Caitlin Smith of the Edmondston-Alston House, Don Bussey and Beth Kerrigan of the Middleton Place Foundation, and Stephanie Thomas and Jennifer McCormick of the Charleston Museum. As always, I am deeply grateful to my editor, Sandy Gilbert Freidus, for expertly guiding this book through every stage, as well as copy editor Kelli Rae Patton for her meticulous editing, and graphic designer Jan Derevjanik for the creativity and patience she brings to the table. And most of all, thanks to Charles Miers, publisher of Rizzoli International Publications, for his ongoing support of my vision as a writer and photographer and his interest in the architecture and design of the South.

RESOURCE GUIDE

HISTORIC HOUSE MUSEUMS

Aiken-Rhett House
historiccharleston.org

Drayton Hall
draytonhall.org

Heyward-Washington House
charlestonmuseum.org

Joseph Manigault House
charlestonmuseum.org

Middleton Place
middletonplace.org

Nathaniel Russell House
historiccharleston.org

ARCHITECTURE

Andrew Gould
newworldbyzantine.com

Beau Clowney Architects
beauclowney.com

Christopher Liberatos
bandlarchitects.com

e e fava architects
eefava.com

Glenn Keyes Architects
glennkeyesarchitects.com

Mark Paullin, AIA
mgpb.com

Richard Marks Restorations
richardmarksrestorations.com

Virginia Dawson Lane
vadlane@gmail.com

INTERIOR DESIGN

Alexandra Howard, Inc.
alexandrahowardinc.com

Amelia T. Handegan, Inc.
athid.com

Athalie Derse Interiors
athaliederseinteriors.com

Ceara Donnelley Ltd. Co.
cearadonnelley.com

Katherine Matthews Interiors
katherinethomasmatthews@gmail.com

Kathleen Rivers
kathleen@kathleenrivers.com

Killian-Dawson Interior Design
killiandawson.com

HISTORIC RESTORATION

Natalie Larson
Historictextile1@aol.com

Susan Buck
paintchipsanalysis@gmail.com

ART

Ann Long Fine Art
annlongfineart.com

George Gallery
georgegalleryart.com

Jason Paul Smith
jasonpaulstudios.com

Karl Beckwith Smith
halcyonplacegallery.com

Mariel Capanna
marielcapanna.com

ANTIQUES

Alexandra
alexandrafrenchantiques.com

Charleston Gardenworks
charlestongardenworks.com

Golden & Associates Antiques
goldenassociatesantiques.com

Tucker Payne Antiques
tuckerpayneantiques.com

FURNITURE

Brown Jordan
brownjordan.com

Jansen Furniture
jansenfurniture.com

Oly Studio
olystudio.com

LIGHTING

Circa Lighting
circalighting.com

Sirmos Lighting
sirmos.com

Stephen Antonson
stephenantonson.com

Urban Electric
urbanelectric.com

TEXTILES AND WALLPAPER

C&C Milano
cec-milano.us

Christopher Hyland Inc.
christopherhyland.com

Claremont
claremontfurnishing.com

de Gournay
degournay.com

Delany and Long Ltd.
delanyandlong.com

Fortuny
fortuny.com

Gracie Studio
graciestudio.com

Holland & Sherry
hollandandsherry.com

Houlès
houles.com

Jasper
michaelsmithinc.com

Lewis & Wood
lewisandwood.co.uk

Michael Devine Ltd.
michaeldevineltd.com

Rogers & Goffigon
rogersandgoffigon.com

Scalamandre
scalamandre.com

Schumacher
fschumacher.com

First published in the United States of America in 2022 by
Rizzoli International Publications, Inc.
300 Park Avenue South
New York, NY 10010
www.rizzoliusa.com

Text and photography © 2022 Susan Sully

Publisher: Charles Miers
Editor: Sandra Gilbert Freidus
Editorial Assistance: Hilary Ney, Kelli Rae Patton,
    Rachel Selekman
Design: Jan Derevjanik
Design Assistance: Olivia Russin
Production Manager: Barbara Sadick
Managing Editor: Lynn Scrabis

Printed in China

2022 2023 2024 2025 / 10 9 8 7 6 5 4 3 2 1

ISBN: 978-0-8478-7157-5
Library of Congress Control Number: 2021948756

VISIT US ONLINE:
Facebook.com/RizzoliNewYork
instagram.com/rizzolibooks
twitter.com/Rizzoli_Books
pinterest.com/rizzolibooks
youtube.com/user/RizzoliNY
issuu.com/Rizzoli